Another Bad-Dog Book

Essays on Life, Love, and Neurotic Human Behavior

Joni B. Cole

D1569006

AffinitySystems
2017

AffinitySystems, Inc.
South Royalton, VT 05068
pubs@affinitysystems.com
LCCN: 2011913641
ISBN-13: 978-0-9753043-2-7
e-Book ISBN: 978-0-9753043-3-4

Cover design: Helmut Baer

Certain essays in this book have appeared
in *Bloodroot Literary Magazine, Image
Magazine, Northern New England Review, the
Valley News, and Woodstock Magazine.*

To Steve, for twenty-five years.

To Esme, good night, I love you, see you in the morning.

To Thea, who makes me happy every day.

Author's Note

I have changed the names and identifying features of some individuals to protect their privacy, and because I don't like it when people are mad at me. Beyond that, these stories are true, albeit my truth, which is sometimes warped.

Contents

ANOTHER BAD-DOG BOOK

Not another one.

I had gone to the bookstore to read the gossip magazines for free when I saw it — yet another best-selling book about someone's adorable, out-of-control dog. Usually these types of bad-dog stories center around a yellow Lab or similar large, loping breed, though the subject of this newest memoir was, according to the title, "a very bad beagle."

The description on the back cover read pretty much the same as all those other bad-dog books that fly off the shelves. The doggie main character was an exuberant, incorrigible scamp with a habit of overturning houseplants, eating table legs, and making madcap dashes through restaurants, offices, and other public venues, all while teaching its owners life lessons like the value of commitment, and what it really means to be a family.

The very bad beagle's mischievous eyes looked up at me from dozens of display copies, all hogging the most precious of real estate in the bookstore—the new release table at the entrance. Just seeing that cute face and those floppy ears, on a hard cover no less, aroused all of my considerable professional jealousy and frustration. *My* new release should have been the one on that front table, that is if I had bothered to write a new release. Unfortunately, my career as an author had not been going so well, at least not since I had discovered the Watch Instantly option on Netflix.

"In this heartwarming and hilarious memoir," I began reading aloud from the cover copy, my voice dripping with disdain.

"I'll be in the music section." My daughter, who had come to the bookstore with me to kill a rainy afternoon, quickly made her escape. This wasn't the first time she'd heard me rant about dog books.

I returned the bad beagle to the table, face down as a form of protest. Of course the store showcased other, equally predictable instant bestsellers: yet another vampire book; another paean to Jane Austen; another celebrity autobiography penned by a ghost writer. Oddly enough, I felt no resentment toward these types of books, maybe because they seemed so far removed from my own realm of interest and ambitions. Vampires? Sure, I'd love to have sex with one, but what's the fun in writing about it? Jane Austen? To me, Jane Austen was like horses, one of those common female obsessions totally lost on me. And celebrity life stories? I fantasized all the time about how great it would be to be a celebrity, specifically a member of the royal family. But if I was a royal, I wouldn't deign to talk to anyone as common as a ghost writer.

But a bad-dog book! As I grabbed some magazines and headed to the café for a Caramocha, it hit me why this breed of book irked me so much. Bad-dog books are the one genre both publishers and readers adore . . . and I should be exploiting.

I have a bad dog. In fact, I've had several bad dogs throughout the years, all of them as incorrigible as any of those troublemakers whose life stories have been made into major motion pictures. What's more, I am a dog person from a long line of dog people on my mother's side of the family. (My father's side, fussy Jews from Romania, are more like plastic slip-cover people.) I'm sure those best-selling bad- dog authors on their fancy book tours endlessly brag about how much they love their pets, but are they dog people like my people? Are they willing to kiss their dogs on the lips, regardless of where those lips have been?

My current bad dog is named Eli, a tiny creature with blackish, fuzzy fur and big, pointy ears. Given that Eli was a stray, his actual pedigree remains a mystery, but he appears to be a disheveled Chihuahua Bat. Eli weighs only nine pounds but has defied our four-hundred-dollar invisible fencing system. One time when I took him to town, he dashed into the open door of a costume designer's studio, and peed on her imported Italian silk fabric. He also scratches a lot (though the fleas have finally been eradicated), and won't let anyone pet our cat in peace. Eli has only lived with our family a short time, but already he has taught us countless life lessons, not the least of which is to forego the idea of carpeting or area rugs for the foreseeable future.

Yet, for all Eli's bad-dog behavior, I love him with all my heart. In fact, on my "Happy List," which I keep taped to my light therapy Sun Box that I use as my desk lamp, I accidentally ranked him above my husband and kids.

And if we're talking about best-selling potential, Eli even has a heartwarming back-story. He was a rescue dog, found wandering the streets of Hartford, Connecticut. After he was picked up and taken to a shelter, the veterinarian who first treated him determined that she needed to pull nine of his little rotten teeth. Unless you happen to be a starving kitten dumped into a library drop box in the middle of a Midwestern snow squall, a back-story doesn't get any better than that.

As I sat in the bookstore's café thinking about my dog and how much more fascinating he was than most celebrities, an idea started to take shape. I pushed aside the gossip magazines I had been skimming, retrieved a notepad from my purse, and began to write.

ELI AND ME
LIFE, LOVE, AND NEUROTIC HUMAN BEHAVIOR

It started with an email from a friend, with a photo enclosed of an adorable little dog perched on an armchair. *Needs a home*, read the message. My friend knew about this dog because one of her co-workers was a rescue-dog volunteer who had been fostering him. My friend also knew that I had been pining for just such a pet, or rather I had been pining for something to cuddle that would love me unconditionally. These were the same simple demands I put on my family and friends, yet all of them constantly disappointed.

The email brought back a recent conversation I'd had with another friend, a woman I particularly appreciated for her ability to listen to me go on and on without trying to get a word in edgewise. We were at a coffee shop in town, talking about mid-life crises, mostly because I suspected I was having one. I couldn't pinpoint any real problems with my life, except lately I had been feeling restless and under-appreciated, and envious of almost every person who crossed my path.

"So after the astrologer read my chart, she told me that this was my *lucky* life." I continued with the story I had been telling my friend. "But when I mentioned this to my sister, she actually laughed in my face."

My friend started telling me about having her chart read, but quickly it became apparent that, similar to how dreams are really only interesting to the person having them, the same goes for astrology readings.

My attention drifted to some teenagers across the street. Five of them were hanging out, smoking near the diner. Smoking was cool, I thought, suddenly craving a cigarette, even though I didn't smoke. Then a really good-looking guy walked by with a dog, which made me crave sex and a cigarette. The dog stayed at his heels even though it wasn't on a leash, suggesting that the man possessed a gentle but commanding authority. For obvious reasons, this only added to his sex appeal.

"I want a dog," I announced, figuring my own sex appeal could use a boost. I hadn't been flirted with in way too long, not counting the mentally impaired guy who hung around town and couldn't articulate words, but always blew me kisses.

My friend gave me a skeptical look. "You don't want a dog," she said. "That's not what you're really looking for."

"Oh yes it is!" I insisted, though I had to admit, this revelation was a surprise even to myself. In truth, I still hadn't quite recovered from our last dog, Lily, who had died four years ago. Lily was a pit bull mix, and the sweetest pet in the world, not withstanding the fact there is a reason why pit bulls are the dog of choice for people with anger issues and knuckle tattoos. While gangbangers might enjoy seeing, say, their neighbor's Pomeranian[1] pinned to the driveway, yipping for its very life, my whitebread nerves couldn't take it.

Lily died at age seventeen, or 119 in people years, though her bladder semi-retired around middle age. While she had the look and constitution of a fireplug, the last three years of her life proved a marathon of near death experiences and miraculous recoveries. Relationship experts claim the number one issue couples argue about is money, but based on personal experience I'd have to say an old dog runs a close second. Neither my husband, Steve, nor I ever wanted Lily to suffer, but our differing sensibilities about when to let her go — me, Never! Steve, about six whopping vet bills ago — made each of her health crises feel like a grudge match between the Pope and Dr. Kevorkian.

I reread the email message on my computer. The dog in the enclosed photograph was so over-the-top adorable it could have been created by one of those Disney animators

---

[1] *The Pomeranian was just fine. I, on the other hand, still have flashbacks.*

who are masters at manipulating emotions using cuteness archetypes. Stick an oversized head on a small pudgy body, throw in some saucer eyes and big, pointy ears, and bam! Instant heart melt. Confronted with this kind of movie magic, no wonder audiences for generations have overlooked the fact that most Disney classics involve some form of matricide.

According to the email message, the dog's name was Cricket, or at least that was the name given to him by the rescue-dog volunteer who was fostering him. This was her second stint as his foster mom; he'd already been returned to the shelter once by a family who had decided not to keep him.

Oh my goodness! Even if I hadn't been so completely taken by his disheveled appearance, and the way his little pink tongue stuck out between his lips, just the concept of "rescue dog"—and a reject, at that—made me want to rise to my better self. I could save this dog! I could turn his life around! Not being the rescuer type, this could make up for a certainty born of countless bad dreams that if ever I was confronted with an actual rescue situation—say someone being descended upon by zombies—I would a) scream, but no sound would come out; b) try to run, except my feet wouldn't move; and c) realize that I wasn't wearing any clothes.

Still, despite the heady rush of imagining myself saving this precious creature, I knew I needed to think things through. First was the obvious question: Did I really want the responsibility of dog ownership? Of course not, but that was hardly a deterrent. More problematic was the fact that Steve was unlikely to want to take care of another dog. This would be a challenge, to convince someone who was more of a dog *tolerator* than a dog person that fur on the furniture and poop in the yard would greatly enhance his life.

And then there were other issues to consider. Like so many people who find themselves with a closet full of Bacon

Genies, Snuggies, and Ronco Rotisseries, I tended to be an impulse shopper, and sometimes those impulses brought home pets. I didn't regret bringing home any of these wonderful creatures; still, the memories weren't all happy ones. In second grade, for example, I acquired a classmate's adorable, albeit rheumy-eyed mouse, and hid it in a shoebox in my closet. My mother discovered my secret pet running around my room while she was cleaning, and blew her stack. Given her affection for animals, the only reason I can fathom for her anger is that she probably thought it would clog her vacuum.

When I was in high school, I brought home a friend's dog because her parents were going to take it to the pound. In those days, everyone understood the pound was just another way of saying doggie death row. In this case, my mother agreed we should take in this shy, wispy blond mutt. What was one more dog when our family already owned three? Tragically, Daisy died just a few months later, after choking on a steak bone she had pulled from the trash.

And then there were the pets I acquired after I reached adulthood. Sherwood, my fluffy white bunny, is what happens when you find yourself single and alone at the King of Prussia mall on yet another dateless Saturday night. It's a certain kind of loneliness that allows you to believe a Pretty Pets salesclerk who insists, "Of course you can house-train a rabbit!"

Shortly after marriage, Steve and I acquired Foo Foo the cat, who originally belonged to our neighbors in graduate student housing. Over time, my campaign of obsessive petting convinced everyone involved that a better home awaited Foo Foo on our side of the duplex. The cat was still with us when Steve and I moved into our current house, an historic cape with a secret closet allegedly used to hide runaway slaves, and a three-hearth fireplace with a built-in beehive oven. Not being the fireplace-stoking-bread-baking-type, I have never been inclined to make use of the oven, but Foo Foo found comfort in it when he needed a place to die.

Eight years into marriage, Steve and I realized we probably should get around to having children. That's when I went to the pet store and brought home Pierre the cockatiel. We kept Pierre's cage in the master bathroom, though he spent considerable time on my shoulder, preening his feathers and dropping bird doo down the back of my shirt. I don't recall Pierre ever causing a bit of trouble, at least not until the day he died, when I caught Steve about to toss his stiffening corpse into the bathroom trash.

By this time, we did have children—two little girls—and one day they decided they wanted pet rats. Ugh. When it came to furry creatures, even I drew the line somewhere. All I could think about were the Ratzillas that used to get into our house, until Steve did something with poison and a hammer that I'd rather not think about.

"We can go to the pet store to *look*," I told my daughters, "but there is no way in hell I'm bringing one of those disgusting things home."

The minute I saw the two baby fancy rats, curled up together in their cage, I was smitten. According to the handbook *Best Pets for Small Children* (conveniently available for browsing in the pet store's rodent room), the rat's black beady eyes belie an innate intelligence and gentle playfulness. How could we not bring Squeakums and Charlie home with us, along with a two-story rat condo, an elaborate play-tube-slash-mega-maze, and just about every other type of rodent accessory imaginable, save for tiny, yellow Live Strong wristbands?

Charlie passed away within two years, marking one of my children's early encounters with grief, not to mention irony, given it was Squeakums who had developed two tumors on his side resembling conjoined Hackey Sacks.

Even so, Squeakums soldiered on and on and on, long after he could no longer squeeze into his mega-maze.

By the time the email about Cricket arrived in my inbox, our family was down to one pet, Milo the cat. I'd brought Milo home a couple Christmases ago, and like every one of my previous pets, I loved him with all my heart. Still, a cat was not a dog.

How old is Cricket? I typed. What would it hurt to ask the rescue-dog volunteer a few questions?

Between two and four, she emailed back. *At least that's the vet's best guess.*

Does he get along with other animals?

Yep.

Children?

Yep.

"Cricket." I said the name aloud. Of course it would have to be changed. Given how I thought of dogs more as surrogate children than pets, it seemed more appropriate to give them human names.

That evening, I showed Cricket's photo to Steve. You would think, given the dog's cuteness, this would have been all the convincing necessary. "Just look at his oversized head," I pointed out. "Check out those saucer eyes."

Steve looked, but apparently was immune to the Disney magic.

"What is it?" he asked, nonplussed. Given his lack of enthusiasm, I knew to choose my next words with care.

"The rescue-dog volunteer said we could bring him home for the weekend." I kept my tone light, casual. "Just a trial run, to see how he fits in with our family. No commitment, of course."

"I don't know . . ." Steve hesitated.

And so it was decided.

By the end of the trial weekend, our family had settled on a new name for Cricket. We agreed to call him Eli, though I quickly babified this to E-Pie-Pie, just as I used to babify names for both my daughters, until they made me stop.

Within days, Eli had bonded with everyone in our family. But like an answered, neurotic prayer, he clearly loved me best. His whole tiny body waggled when he saw me. During the day, he followed me from room to room, and at night he burrowed under the covers on my side of the bed, like a fuzzy hot-water bottle warming my feet. In the car, Eli rested on my lap, his head tucked between his paws, just clearing the underside of the steering wheel.

Toward the end of the week the girls and I took Eli shopping for a doggie sweater and toys. I made him an appointment at the groomer for a haircut and blueberry facial. To my mind, Eli was already my dog, as much a part of our family, no, more so, than some of Steve's closest relatives.

Meanwhile, the only contact I'd had with the rescue-dog volunteer was a brief email exchange after the trial weekend, in which I told her how much I loved "Cricket."

Great! she wrote back.

That's why it was such a shock when she sent me another email on Friday, telling me I needed to return him. Apparently, another family had visited the rescue-dog's website and filled out an application to adopt him. Because I hadn't completed the paperwork, the organization's director assumed Cricket was still available, and promised him to this other family.

No, no, no! I shot back an email. *No, no, no!*

I'm so sorry, the rescue-dog volunteer responded. *The shelter operates on a first-come-first-served basis. You can hurry up and fill out an application online, but we're already checking the other family's references.*

I found the rescue-dog operation's website and hastily

completed the adoption form. Then I checked my email, hoping for a miraculously fast response to my application. Because I was at my computer, I figured I should work on a writing assignment, but all I could think about was Eli. I looked at him resting on his new fleece pillow, so content. What if the rescue dog volunteer wrote back with bad news? Was I really going to let another family take him?

I thought of all those Lifetime movies where the mothers take their children on the lam to avoid sharing custody with their serial murderer spouses. Those women may have had seriously bad taste in men, but they also had guts! And then there were those other mothers you read about in the newspapers who instantly develop super human strength to lift cars off their children. If I had super powers, I thought, opening a new file on the computer, I could use them to save Eli, and that would only be for starters.. . . .

THE ADVENTURES OF SUPER JONI!
(AND HER AMAZING DOG E-PIE-PIE)

PART ONE: *THE DARING RESCUE*

Super Joni was naturally blond, blue-eyed, and remarkably youthful for her age. By day, she was self-actualized. By night, she never succumbed to sugar cravings, or watched Netflix for hours on end. Super Joni lived a life of quiet domesticity in an old house (old in a good way) with her husband and two daughters. But she was also one of the most famous people in the world. In fact, she was a royal!

Ping!

One day, an urgent message popped up on Super Joni's electronic hotline, which she checked compulsively in case someone, anyone, needed her. A little disheveled dog with nine bad teeth and saucer eyes was in trouble at the animal shelter!

Super Joni applied some makeup (even though she really didn't need any), slid on her skinny jeans, which were never too tight, whipped up a nourishing casserole for her family's dinner that night, and was out the door in less than five minutes.

"Super Joni to the rescue!" cried the royal watchers who followed her every move, but always kept a respectable distance. Super Joni waved to her adoring public as she sped away in her Prius. (Not only was she a champion of homeless dogs, but of the environment, too!)

Just in the knick of time, Super Joni arrived at the animal shelter. An Evil Rescue-Dog Volunteer was about to hand over the little, disheveled dog to an unsuitable family with a toddler. The toddler's dimpled hands clenched and unclenched in anticipation of playing too rough.

"Stop!" Super Joni commanded. "The little, disheveled dog stays with me!"

"You're too late!" The Evil Rescue-Dog Volunteer brandished a completed adoption application. "Our policy is first come, first served!" But even before Super Joni had developed super powers, she had never been afraid to cut in line.

Jab! Jab! Zumba!

With a mix of high cardio kickboxing and Latin dance moves, Super Joni overpowered the Evil Rescue-Dog Volunteer (and burned 1,429 calories in the process). Quickly, she locked the woman in a dog crate with a very bad beagle who promptly ate the completed application.

"You'll never get away with this!" cried the Evil Rescue-Dog Volunteer. "I'll have my revenge."

But Super Joni was not to be intimidated. She gave the unsuitable family with the toddler a pit bull mix, and sent them on their way. Then she picked up the little, disheveled dog and cuddled him.

"From now on, your name shall be E-Pie- Pie," she said softly. The dog's pointy ears perked up; his saucer eyes brimmed with love and gratitude. Already, Super Joni knew that he loved her unconditionally, just like all of her friends and family.

PART TWO: *NOWHERE TO HIDE*

It was late at night. Super Joni's husband and two daughters were sound asleep in their beds by the time she stumbled home from a party. E-Pie- Pie greeted her happily and off they went to the kitchen to reheat some pizza. The house was quiet, too quiet, or maybe Super Joni just wanted some action.

A strange noise sounded at the front door. Look there! Super Joni peeked through the glass. A suspicious looking mini-van sat parked across the darkened street. It must belong to the Evil Rescue- Dog Volunteer! Who else would drive such a gas guzzler! And given the van comfortably seated seven, she likely had brought accomplices.

Super Joni knew she needed to hide E-Pie-Pie, and fast!

Bam. Crash. Clunk.

Super Joni emptied a hall closet stuffed with products as seen on TV—Bacon Genies, Snuggies, Ronco Rotisseries. There was that Abdominal Cruncher she'd bought for her husband on his birthday! Once cleared of years' worth of accumulated junk, the back of the closet revealed a secret hideaway, rumored to have once been used to shelter runaway slaves.

Super Joni placed E-Pie-Pie and his fleece pillow in the hideaway. My goodness, she thought, barely squeezing out of the tiny enclosure. Either people were a lot smaller in the old days, or the previous owners had lied about this house being part of the Underground Railroad.

Footsteps sounded in the next room! Quickly, Super Joni flicked off the lights, and waited to make her move.

"Ouch! What the #%?!! . . . ?"

The lights flicked back on. Super Joni's husband stood in the hallway, rubbing his big toe, which he had stubbed on the Ab Cruncher. He surveyed the junk-strewn hallway. Given how Super Joni and her husband had been married for a very, very long time, she knew exactly what he must be thinking—*Yay! My Ab Cruncher. Now I can start doing sit-ups again!*

Scratch. Scratch. Itch.

Oh no! If E-Pie-Pie didn't stop scratching, his hiding spot was sure to be discovered! Super Joni's husband looked at the small door inside the emptied closet, then back to Super Joni. "I don't suppose you want to tell me," he shook his head and sighed, "why you've stuck the dog in the slave hideaway?"

And that's when Super Joni knew, no matter how carefully she might try to hide E-Pie-Pie from the Evil Rescue-Dog Volunteer, he would never be safe in this house.

Outside, a sliver of moon silhouetted the mini van still parked across the street. Super Joni retrieved her super-powered eyeglasses and surveilled it through the window. On second thought, she realized, she had seen this van before. Maybe it belonged to the royal watchers . . .or the neighbors, who owned one just like it?

At the door, the strange noise sounded again! Joni flung it open, and in sauntered Milo the cat.

PART THREE: *ON THE LAM! AND OTHER LIFE LESSONS*

For E-Pie-Pie, life on the lam meant freedom from the Evil Rescue-Dog Volunteer. For Super Joni, it meant travel, adventure, romance, and room service. Back home, her family completely understood that this escape from quiet domesticity was simply in response to a crisis, and in no way a reflection on them.

One afternoon, Super Joni and E-Pie-Pie were getting haircuts and blueberry facials at a five-star hotel spa in Aspen or Oslo or Luanda. Anyway, it was one of those places where no ordinary person could afford to live, but Super Joni was no ordinary person.

♫♫♫ (Theme to Swan Lake) ♫♫♫

Suddenly, the ringtone sounded on Super Joni's mobile hotline. She read the caller ID: EVIL RESCUE-DOG VOLUNTEER.

"How did you get this number?!" Super Joni demanded.

"I've kidnapped your entire family," the Evil Rescue-Dog Volunteer exclaimed. "Bring me the little, disheveled dog or else."

Super Joni wasn't born yesterday. "My entire family?" She laughed without mirth. "I doubt you'd last five minutes in a room with all my relatives."

"Bring me the dog," repeated the Evil Rescue-Dog Volunteer, "or you'll never see your precious husband and daughters again!"

Faster than you can say "freebies," Super Joni snatched all the amenities in her hotel suite, including the plush robes. As she and E-Pie-Pie raced home in the Prius, she reflected on her life on the lam. It had been good—no, great—while it lasted, but now that she was in danger of losing her family, nothing seemed to matter but seeing them again!

The Prius silently coasted into the animal shelter parking lot. Super Joni watched and waited. Suddenly, the very bad beagle bolted out the door, while the Evil Rescue-Dog

Volunteer struggled to hold onto his leash. The woman's furtive glances confirmed that either she was hiding something (or someone!) nearby, or she wasn't planning to clean up after her dog.

Super Joni waited until the very bad beagle had dashed around the corner then hurried into the shelter. But before she could find her family, the Evil Rescue-Dog Volunteer had returned!

Bark! Howl! Thud!

The very bad beagle, excited to see a visitor, greeted Super Joni by knocking her backwards with his muddy paws. She fell and bumped her head hard on a Kong Extreme. The next thing she knew, she was seeing stars. The Evil Rescue-Dog Volunteer, seeing her chance, seized the indestructible chew toy and raised her arm to strike a deadly blow . . .

"Yip! Yip! Yap!"

Like a rabid Chihuahua Bat, E-Pie-Pie flew into the room. He nipped at the Evil Rescue-Dog Volunteer's heels and elbows. The very bad beagle started chasing him, thinking it was a game. Then a yellow Lab loped into the room, followed by another dog, and another . . . All the bad dogs had chewed through their kennels!

To escape the mayhem, the Evil Rescue-Dog Volunteer locked herself into a dog crate and called the police to come get her. Meanwhile, E-Pie-Pie sniffed out his family in a back room, and pawed open the door. Once freed, Super Joni's husband and daughters gathered around her, tearfully begging her not to die like all those mothers in Disney movies.

Satisfied with this outpouring of love and attention, Super Joni returned to her senses. Now, more than ever, she

understood the value of commitment and what it really meant
to be a family. As Super Joni and her family hugged, E-Pie-
Pie wreaked havoc and frolicked with all the other bad dogs.
Never before, thought Super Joni, had she witnessed anything
so heartwarming and hilarious.

Outside, the royal watchers waved and cheered! Now this,
they thought, would make a good story!

The End

In what seemed like an eternity (but in reality was only a
few hours), the rescue-dog volunteer emailed me back with
good news. The director of the shelter had decided our family
could keep Cricket, as she still referred to Eli. Despite my
late application, it only made sense. The dog was already
settled in our home, so why put him through another tran-
sition. I also suspected that the rescue-dog volunteer, who
was actually a very nice person, had convinced the director
that this particular applicant was in need of rescuing herself.

So here we were, Eli and me, ready to take on the world.
Maybe it was simply the thrill of victory, but I felt happier
than I had in months. Was it a coincidence, I wondered, that
when I had first started thinking about getting a dog, this
was the very one I had envisioned—small and adorable,
unwavering in his devotion, and a source of heat for my
perpetually cold hands and feet. It was as if I had conjured
up Eli from my very own heart, and fate had delivered him
to me in the form of electronic messaging.

"You don't want a dog," I remembered my friend at the
coffee shop advising me.

Of course I knew what she had been getting at, though I
purposely chose to ignore her real meaning. She had been
trying to tell me that it wasn't a dog I wanted so much as a
safeguard against the darker side of mid-life: that waning

sense of possibility as your choices diminish and your looks fade; the ache of watching your kids need you less and less; the restlessness that can infect even a good life and marriage, if only because change seems more exciting, and you want it all.

My friend's wisdom wasn't lost on me. I had heard it all before from other reliable sources, and it all made perfect sense. Real happiness comes from within. You can't rely on anyone else to make you feel good about yourself. You're only lonely when you don't like the person you're alone with. Eli watched me from his fleece pillow at my feet. As always, the tip of his pink tongue peeked out from between his lips. Just seeing how cute and happy he looked made me smile.

I understood how it might seem naïve to think a dog could help someone through a mid-life crisis. And yet, just the fact that Eli loved me so much somehow made me feel more lovable. I also understood that, if there were times in life when I felt like an abyss of need, I couldn't expect others to fill the void. Still, I thought, picking up Eli and cuddling him in my lap, a little, nine-pound dog with saucer eyes could come pretty close.

WINNING WOMEN

I had so wanted to look nice.

I was flying to St. Louis to give two talks—one to a business organization called Winning Women, and one to the Junior Girl Scouts of Southeastern Missouri. The irony of being invited to address women executives and ten-year-old girls who earned badges for community service was not lost on me. I have never been able to hold a job for more than two years, and my last civic duty was glaring at a smoker outside Applebee's. But I had authored a few books, and this accomplishment obscured a multitude of failings.

To make up for my lack of suitability as a motivational speaker, not to mention months of neglecting my personal appearance, I was committed to making an effort.

Most of my effort started twenty-four hours before my flight. I decided to color my fading, yellow hair, partly because it seemed ungracious to fly my graying roots halfway across the country on someone else's tab, and partly because I wanted to look fifteen years younger.

Usually when I dye my hair, I choose the medium blond shade of a product called Natural Match. But wasn't "medium" just another way of saying "average," a shade for women who not only didn't win much, but didn't even like competition and choked at the first sign of it? Yes, that was me, but I didn't need to advertise it. So I decided to go with a "warmer" blond tone, thinking I would coordinate my hair color with the arrival of summer. Maybe it would even create the illusion of a sunny disposition.

At first I was hoping it was just bad lighting. But when I looked at my newly dyed hair in the bathroom mirror, and then in every other mirror in the house, and on the visor of our Prius, it was still there—a distinctly brassy hue.

This was not the kind of brass associated with top military personnel or expensive floor lamps. This was the kind of brass that brought to mind a boy I'll call Joey Delong, and his dented trumpet. Joey Delong was last chair of the brass section in my high school band. Because I was the worst flute player in band, my own chair sat adjacent to Joey's, our spit-filled embouchures creating a discord of windy toots, blasts, and wrong notes. Plus, Joey Delong was a hoodlum. Once at an away game, he got drunk and threw up in my open flute case.

I retrieved the discarded box of hair dye from the bathroom trash. There was my mistake, explained on an overlooked three-dollars-off coupon good toward my next purchase of Natural Match. *Choose a warmer formula to add RED tones* read the copy on the coupon. Oh no, I realized, a second grader could have predicted this disastrous outcome. My pre-existing hair color was yellow. The "warmer" dye added red tones. Yellow plus red equals orange.

The next part of my effort had to do with my legs. Five long winter months of no exposure to the sun, blast-furnace heat, and being too lazy to moisturize had left my skin the color and texture of moon rock. If I was to expose my calves beneath a skirt without the inconvenience of nylons, I would need a tan. Specifically, a fake tan, which I had purchased in an aerosol can at CVS earlier that day, at the same time I picked up the hair dye.

Learning from past mistakes, this time I made a point to read the instructions, including the copy on the inserts. *Spray the tanning lotion on your palm then quickly and evenly apply it to your skin to avoid streaking.* I aimed the can's pinhole toward my palm. A mound of poo-colored foam peaked in my hand. No time to reconsider, I started rubbing it into my legs.

But no matter which way I rubbed—in sweeping up- and-down strokes and then frantic, concentric circles—the fake tan wouldn't apply evenly. Parts of my legs remained light, while other parts were smeared dark brown, like the walls next to the crib of some deranged, diaper-less baby. The more foam I applied, the darker the streaks. In desperation, I skipped the first step of spraying the foam into my palm, and aimed it directly at the remaining patches of moon rock.

A few minutes later I emerged from the bathroom. This was not the look I had hoped for—middle-school-band atop feces. Perhaps, I thought ruefully, I should have started my effort sooner. Perhaps this effort should have included an appointment with a hair care *professional*, and a visit to one of those trendy spray-tan places where you're misted with a bronze glow, then patted down by an attendant. I had read an article recently about how movie stars get spray-on tans before they appear at award shows. At the time, I wondered about the safety of spraying chemical dyes directly into your pores. A mental picture formed of Charlize Theron and Nicole Kidman on the Red Carpet, waving to their fans, only instead of arms they had flippers. Things could always be worse, I told myself, trying to maintain some perspective. At least I didn't have spray-tan appendages.

At the airport, my confidence plummeted even further. The infrequent times I fly, I usually travel in jeans, but today I wore a loose black skirt and a stretchy white wrap shirt. A simple, stylish outfit, I thought that morning when I extracted it from my closet; an outfit for the contemporary winning woman on the go.

Who was I kidding? I thought now, waiting at the boarding

gate and eating a cruller. These were my fat clothes. The past year of deadlines, doughnuts, and delusional thinking that I could still eat anything I wanted without consequences, had taken its toll on my middle. My skirt had an elastic waistband. My shirt's front pleats were designed to camouflage two stomach rolls that rippled over the waistband of my Spanx Thigh-Shaper panties like a capital B.

I caught myself scowling at the petite Japanese business-woman in line in front of me. She wore a tailored navy suit and a Bluetooth peeking out from her sleek, black hair. Even her carry-on luggage was trim, a fashionable powder-blue case on wheels. You never see fat Japanese women, I thought, adjusting my own lumpy shoulder bag like a pack saddle on a donkey. They're always slim and feminine-looking, and probably don't even have a word for Spanx. It occurred to me, if I ever traveled to Japan, I would be the fattest woman in the entire country, a country of 127 million people.

On the plane, things went from bad to worse. I spent most of the flight going over my Winning Women speech, which I had spent weeks writing and rewriting, and practicing in front of my reluctant husband and children. Because public speaking terrifies me, I had overcompensated by scripting every word and stage direction—"Hello." *(Smile!)* "It's a pleasure to be here." *(Stand up straight, and have fun!)*

At some earlier point in time, I remembered liking my speech, but now it seemed silly and trite, an Up-With- People message, only I was the opposite of a perky, talented teenager. I could just see it now: a roomful of three-hundred Winning Women, all pretending to listen to me, but secretly multitask-ing. Five minutes into my fifty-minute talk, the organization's president would usher me away from the podium.

"So sorry," she'd say, pausing to check email on her Blackberry, "but our organization is committed to work-life balance, and I'm afraid you don't qualify as quality time."

I put my speech away, intending to relax, but then I splattered coffee down the front of my white shirt. In the lavatory, I saturated a bunch of Wet Knaps in the undrinkable water and managed to soak out the stains, but we were landing in less than an hour. The stretchy fabric over my breasts was covered with big, wet blotches. Whoever was meeting me at the airport would think I was lactating, like one of those women you read about in the tabloids who have babies freakishly late in life. "Middle-aged author delivers quintuplets!"

When I returned to my seat, no one seemed to notice that I was wearing what amounted to a skin-tight, see-through, soaking-wet t-shirt. At first I was relieved, but then it occurred to me — why hadn't anyone noticed, not even the young guy in the seat beside me? He was watching an action-adventure movie on his iPod, the kind of movie that specializes in gratuitous violence and objectifying women. Yet here I was, only an armrest away, my cold nipples protruding so far they were practically sitting in first class, and it was like I was invisible. No, I didn't want people staring at my breasts. But I did want breasts that people would want to stare at, if that sort of thing wasn't frowned upon.

Now wouldn't that be a fine message for the Junior Girl Scouts, I thought. One of the Winning Women (who was also a Girl Scout leader) had asked me to serve as one of their role model speakers at their regional meeting. The girls were earning their Career Badges, so I was to talk about my job and offer inspiration.

"You can be anything you want to be!" I would tell the Junior Girl Scouts. "But what difference does it make if you can't even get noticed in a wet t-shirt?"

By the time the plane arrived in St. Louis, my confidence was completely shot. I started humping my carry-on sack toward baggage claim, all the other arriving and departing passengers only serving to remind me of my own insignificance. The petite Asian woman with the powder-blue case was long gone. No baggage claim for her, given her entire tiny corporate wardrobe could fit on the head of a pin.

Near the luggage carousel, I spotted one of the Winning Women holding up a sign with my name on it. She looked to be in her early thirties, and probably had two-point-five children and ran a Fortune 100 company. No doubt she was super nice, too, which only made things worse. She glanced around the crowded carousel, but didn't see me, or more likely didn't recognize me from the picture on my website. And why should she? I thought. At the time the photo was taken, I didn't look like a spray-tanned Joey Delong.

At that moment, I wished with all my heart that I had never agreed to be a guest speaker for Winning Women. I wished that I hadn't promised to be a role model for the Junior Girl Scouts of Southeastern Missouri. But it was too late for that kind of thinking. I had committed to making an effort. It was time to earn my own badge of courage.

I walked over to the woman holding the sign with my name on it, and introduced myself.

"Hello." *(Smile!)* "It's a pleasure to be here." *(Stand up straight and have fun!)*

BEST FRIENDS FOREVER

"My husband is my best friend!" I am always hearing women say this, both in real life and on celebrity talk shows, but I just can't fathom what they're talking about. I mean, I love my husband. Steve and I have been married a thousand years, and I have no plans on leaving him any time soon (as if I could even afford it). But my best friend? I have lots of different best friends, depending on my mood, but these are all women or gay men who enjoy eating my root vegetable soups and watching Colin Firth movies, and who are willing to gossip with me for hours, usually about our husbands. If your husband is your best friend, how do you gossip about him?

The last time someone bragged to me, "My husband is my best friend," it got me worrying. Maybe there's something wrong with my husband and me, I thought. Maybe there's something *lacking* in our relationship. That night I couldn't sleep so I decided to distract myself by reading my novel in bed. I actually prefer sleeping with the lights on, but Steve likes it dark. He lay beside me, a motionless mound under the covers. I silently rolled over and tapped the base of my bedside lamp to turn it on low. Steve jolted upright as if he'd been tasered.

"What's wrong?!!" he asked. "What's the matter?" When Steve was in his early twenties, he was a live-in counselor at a residential juvenile detention facility. One night he woke to the smell of smoke, managed to rouse the delinquents, and escorted them all to safety. Ever since then he's been a light sleeper, primed for catastrophe, even when sound asleep.

"Nothing's wrong," I said, irritated. "I'm going downstairs to read."

Downstairs, I turned on the overhead light and sulked on the living room couch, begrudging the fact that we need to keep the thermostat turned down at night to save on heating costs. Too antsy to read, I flipped through TV channels. At the moment, it seemed the only remotely watchable show was the movie *Fun with Dick and Jane*, a far-fetched comedy about a married couple who falls on hard times after Dick (played by Jim Carrey) loses his job. In response, he and his wife Jane (played by Téa Leoni) resort to robbing convenience stores and banks. Despite devastating financial hardship and the usual challenges inherent in a life of federal crime, Dick and Jane manage to have even more fun together. Yet another one of those annoying BFF couples.

By now it was 2:17 a.m. and I had wound myself up, thinking about all the ways my husband and I weren't best friends: how we had nothing in common (children don't count), and how we were going to end up in just a few short years like so many other empty nesters who look at each other across the middle cushion of their corduroy couch and think, *Wow. What now? Why am I with this person? I hate corduroy.* Clearly, not only were Steve and I not best friends, we were completely incompatible. I ticked off a mental checklist:

1. I live in fear of people getting all emotional. Steve is a mental health professional.

2. When Steve does the laundry, he folds the underwear. Am I supposed to spend my life folding underwear, as if I have nothing better to do?

3. We don't even use the same coffeepot because Steve thinks my pumpkin spice coffee pollutes his precious gold filter.

Why did we ever get married? I glared at the TV. Why can't Steve be more like Jim Carrey? Why can't I look more like Téa Leoni? Why can't we go to my favorite Chinese restaurant in town and share the sushi-for-two platter?

"Oh, try this one, darling. It's eel," I would say. "Here, let me feed it to you off my chopsticks."

If Steve was my best friend, if we were really meant for each other, he wouldn't hate sushi. He would eat eel off my chopsticks and like it.

I heard footsteps on the stairs. Now what? I thought. Was the TV too loud? I tugged my flannel nightshirt over my bare knees. I hate being shushed. My husband has said to me on more than one occasion, "You don't have to shout. I'm right here," at which point, I usually accommodate him by giving him the silent treatment. One of these days, I made up my mind, I was going to live in my own over- heated apartment and sleep with all the lights on. And I was going to talk as loud as I wanted!

Steve shuffled into the living room. He was carrying the red comforter from our bed in a bundled-up ball. His salt-and-pepper hair was mashed against one side of his head.

"I thought you might need this." He plopped the comforter on my lap then headed for the kitchen. I watched him go in his faded Life is Good t-shirt and plaid boxers. Still half asleep, he opened the fridge, stared inside it for a few moments, then closed the door and headed back up the stairs to bed.

And just like that, my marriage was saved.

I spread the red comforter over my legs and pulled it up to my chin. Maybe Steve and I don't have a ton of things in common, I thought, as I clicked off the TV and closed my eyes in our brightly lit living room. I smiled, thinking about him coming downstairs to check up on me, like he always does, even in his sleep. Maybe Steve and I weren't the kind of couple who always prefers each other's company and never runs out of things to say. But he keeps me warm in the middle of the night, and whenever I get all emotional, no one knows better how to make things right.

A REAL BOZO

For once, some good news in the morning headlines.Bozo the clown has died. Even as a kid, I couldn't stand clowns, and still fail to see the humor in white-faced men with giant tufts of flame-colored hair sprouting from the sides of their head. Whereas mimes, by comparison, are just peculiar (what type of aspiring entertainer thinks, *I know, I'll pretend to be mute and stuck in a box?*), I believe clowns cross the line into creepy. The red, bulbous nose. The huge shoes. The way they're always contorting balloons into wiener dogs. Whenever I see a clown in real life or on TV, I always want to ask, "Why bother with all that symbolism and pretense? Why not just come out and say, 'Hey boys and girls! Look at me. I'm a drunk with an exaggerated view of my manhood. Do you find my suggestive costuming as amusing as I do?'"

It turned out that the headline in the paper that day wasn't really about the death of Bozo the Clown, but rather Larry Harmon, the actor who played Bozo on TV for fifty years, and bought the copyright to the character in the 1950s. The article described eighty-three-year-old Larry Harmon as "beloved," and I'm sure his family and friends, and all those people who weren't traumatized by clowns as children, still smile fondly at the memory of his size 83AAA shoes. But that morning when my then eight-year-old daughter interrupted my reading of Larry Harmon's obituary to ask me if she could have an end-of-summer party, I knew one thing for sure. We wouldn't be hiring any clowns for the event.

"Are you sure you want a party?" I folded the newspaper and tucked a loose strand of her long brown hair behind her ear. I always get nervous when my kids want to host parties, not because they aren't well liked, but because I wasn't popular as a kid. One time in elementary school I was standing at the bus port when a classmate, Kelly Walls, came up to me and told me that I was the *ugliest* girl in school.

What?!

I knew with my fat cheeks and buck teeth that I was no Peggy Lipton, but the ugliest girl in school? For years, I'd catch myself debating the point in my head. What about Kathy Brubaker? I'd argue. With her home-spun dresses and coiled braids, she looked just like one of those polygamist wives, even when she was ten. What about the speds? I'd reason. Those kids had to be sequestered in their own specially equipped classrooms. What about Kelly Walls herself? I'd demand, the voice in my head growing ever more strident. Just because Kelly was inexplicably popular didn't make that red birthmark on her neck any more pleasant to look at.

Now, of course, over thirty years later, I know enough to understand that when Kelly Walls told me that I was the ugliest girl in school, she was probably projecting her own insecurities onto me. I also know that it is cruel to refer to students with developmental disorders as speds, let alone sequester them in a remote part of the school. But still, I felt a sudden, familiar surge of defensiveness—*the ugliest girl in school?*

"I want it to be a water party," my daughter said, interrupting my thoughts, while ducking out of reach to prevent me from fussing with her hair. Sadly, she had recently moved into the "No More Babying" phase. Until a few months ago, I had been able to mom-handle her any time I wanted, whereas now I had to curb, or at least negotiate, any kind of physical affection.

"Okay," I looked at her, wishing the brown spots on my face looked as cute in the morning sun as the sprinkling of freckles across her nose. "You can have a party . . . if you give me a hug."

Over the next couple weeks, my daughter winnowed down her guest list to six best friends, and we loaded up on squirt guns and other water-party supplies. The morning of the event, she came downstairs already dressed in her bikini, and handed me a piece of a paper. At the top she'd printed — *Mommy's Dos and Don'ts!*

"What's this?" I asked.

"It's a list," she explained, "so you know how to act at the party."

I read the first instruction — *Do not say I love you.* "What's the matter with saying I love you?" I demanded. "You say it all the time," she answered. "And you say it to my friends."

"I do not," I argued.

"Yes, you do," my other daughter chimed in. Yesterday, the girls had been fighting over who was better at petting the cat, but today, presented with the opportunity to conduct an intervention on my parental shortcomings, they were a miraculously united front.

The list continued: *Do not follow people around. Do not do your pig impersonation.*

"I don't even have a pig impersonation!" I said, prompting both my daughters to wrinkle their noses and start snuffling, a mockery of that special funny face I had entertained them with since they were newborns. Of course, until this moment, I'd never thought of it as pig-like.

I flipped the paper over to the list of Dos. According to my daughter I was permitted to *1. Ask about people's summers; 2. Use a water gun; 3. Use the Slip 'N Slide.*

"Sorry, Mom," she said, no doubt reacting to my stony

silence. "Are you okay?" If my daughter's early education at private kindergarten had taught her anything, it was that you should talk about your feelings and encourage others to do so as well.

"I'm fine," I waved her off. "I won't act like a pig at your party." Our cat was lounging on a nearby kitchen chair and I tried to pick him up to nuzzle his fur, but he darted away, probably still traumatized after yesterday's bout of competitive petting.

At the party, five girls and one boy ran around the yard, assaulting each other with water balloons and taking turns on the Slip 'N Slide. To give them some semblance of privacy, my husband and I placed our lawn chairs at the far end of the yard, where Steve could read the newspaper in peace, and I could have a glass of wine and eavesdrop without being obvious.

As the party moved from the water games to the munchies table, the children's conversation shifted to secret crushes and school gossip. Their conversation reinforced that, even though these kids were only eight or nine years old, their exposed tummies still rounded in a way that, sadly, only looks adorable on children, they were growing up fast. Any day now, I thought, my kids would hand me more lists with more Dos and Don'ts—*Do not touch us; Do not speak to us*—until eventually they would take out a restraining order and that would be that.

One of the kids cranked up the music on the CD player, and they all started playing Twister on the porch. Seeing their youthful, entangled bodies made me yearn for some physical contact; the warmth of a human touch. It also made me painfully aware of how I would look if I were to play Twister in a bikini. I thought about looping my arm through Steve's, or making him hold my hand, but he was absorbed in the newspaper's crossword puzzle. No doubt he would indulge my affections for a few minutes, and then manufacture some excuse, like needing to pencil in six down, to extricate himself from my hot, sweaty palm.

By now, maybe because of the pressure not to make my pig face, or maybe because I don't do well in the sun with a glass of wine in my system, I was feeling rather weepy and morose. Forget about children who grow up and see you as an embarrassment, I thought. Forget about husbands and their hand-holding charity. Forget about cats, too. I watched ours dart across the backyard, no doubt intending to kill some poor, pathetic creature, but only after making it suffer.

As I wallowed in my gloom, an idea occurred to me. I would get myself a dog, I decided, a lap dog that would be all mine and no one else's, except for in the mornings and evenings when Steve would have to walk it. And this lapdog—maybe I would call it Pootchiegoo or Pootchies for short—would have soft, charcoal fur and big eyes, and he would live for my hugs and kisses.

Eventually, the kids abandoned their game of Twister and started running around the yard again, squirting each other with the hose. My daughter dashed over to me to ask if I would fetch more towels. Her pretty face radiated happiness and I almost slipped and said, "I love you," but caught myself just in time. When I get Pootchiegoo, I thought, traipsing up the stairs to the bathroom, I will tell him that I love him all the time, and he will wag his cute tail, and make those little yippy noises I taught him that sound remarkably similar to, "I wuv you, too."

In the bathroom, I grabbed some towels then took a moment to check my appearance in the mirror. I look ridiculous, I thought. My straw-colored hair frizzed out beneath my baseball cap, and my face had a whitish cast from the sun block cream, except for my red nose, which always managed to get sunburned. Heading back to the party, my flip flops smacked on the stairs. *Flip. Flop. Flip. Flop.*

And that's when it occurred to me. *Flip. Flop. Flip. Flop.* This must be how my kids see me all the time, the same way I see Bozo the Clown and his size 83AAA shoes.

Outside, the party-goers eventually grew tired of their water games and spread their towels on a dry patch of lawn, luxuriating in the late afternoon sun. Steve had retreated into the house and I started tidying up the yard. The hose had been turned off, but the Slip 'N Slide remained slick with grass-filled water. I remembered my daughter's list of Dos, which included this activity.

"Hey, boys and girls, look at me!" I imagined myself call-ing out to the party-goers, as I dove onto the slide head first, skimming its surface on my belly. "Aren't I hilarious? Do you want to be my pal?" But of course this would have been more creepy than funny. So I continued with my clean-up, picking up bits of balloon pieces scattered across the yard, like a massacre of wiener dogs the children had already forgotten.

OH, DIDN'T I TELL YOU?

I've recently started watching the Showtime series *Queer as Folk* on DVD, and now I can't seem to stop watching it. The series originally aired between 2000 and 2005, and revolves around four, thirty-something gay friends in Pittsburgh who have sex with their partners and total strangers about ninety times a day, in between dealing with life's daily dramas.

Will Michael, the adorable, comic-book-loving "boy-next-door," come out to his co-workers at the Big Q-Mart? Will Brian, the gorgeous advertising executive, use his considerable creative talents to help the homophobic police chief get elected as mayor? Will Teddy, the doe-eyed accountant — and the last one anyone would peg as a drug user — be able to beat his addiction to crystal meth? And last but hardly least, will Emmett, dear, funny, flamboyant Emmett, ever find true love (and not with that hypocritical, engaged-to-a-woman pro-football star who is clearly just using him for sex)?

In many ways, Emmett reminds me of my best friend from college who also was gay and funny and lived in Pittsburgh. Emmett, however, favors fishnet shirts and works as a party planner, while my friend Jeff preferred polo shirts with the collar turned up, and worked as the editor of *Out*, Pittsburgh's gay and lesbian newspaper.

A few weeks ago, Jeff phoned me out of the blue to catch up. We only talk every few years, but he's still one of my favorite people for all the same reasons that Emmett's friends love him for his big heart and fabulous wit. As soon as I hear Jeff's voice on the phone, I automatically smile.

Jeff and I graduated from college in the '80s at Indiana University of Pennsylvania, located in Indiana, Pennsylvania, the hometown of the actor Jimmy Stewart, and supposedly the inspiration for Bedford Falls in *It's a Wonderful Life*. This was not the best recommendation for two restless college kids who loved disco and Donna Summer, and shared the same career aspiration—to one day write for *People* magazine.

Jeff loved the story of the first day we met at a meeting for journalism majors our freshman year. I don't even remember this interaction, but, as Jeff tells it, he asked me for a piece of paper, so I ripped off a tiny corner of a page from my notebook and handed him, literally, a piece of paper. Who knows why, but Jeff thought this was funny, and maybe I was trying to be funny. Or maybe I just didn't have any paper to spare.

Before Jeff came out to me, or to anyone at our school, he dated my roommate, Debbie. Despite the fact that both he and I were going out with other people, this didn't stop us from spending most of our time together. We made a point to take the same classes, and wrote each other sentimental notes—*You're my best friend forever . . . I'd be lost without you!* In truth, Jeff and I so preferred each other's company that we often alienated our other friends, not unlike Michael and Brian in *Queer as Folk*, who have been best friends since they were teenagers and truly love each other, just not in that way.

By our junior year of college, Jeff had broken up with Debbie and started spending a lot of weekends in Pittsburgh, which was about two hours—and a universe—away from Jimmy Stewart's hometown. Jeff told me he shared an apartment in the city with some guy he knew from high school who was a couple years older than us. On Saturday nights, they usually went dancing at a disco named Heaven. One weekend, Jeff asked me to come along with him to Pittsburgh. His roommate was going to be out of town so we could have the apartment to ourselves. When we arrived, Jeff fixed us each a rum and Diet Coke. Then he put a Donna Summer album on the stereo and went into the bedroom to change. I rummaged through some magazines stacked on the coffee table: *GQ, People,* and several unfamiliar publications that showed a lot of shirtless men in provocative poses, most of them young Richard Gere clones.

When Jeff came out of the bedroom, he was wearing his tightest pair of Levi jeans with, as he liked to brag, a 29-inch waist. The sleeves of his white shirt were rolled up above his biceps, and he had slicked back his recently permed hair with gel.

"Jeff," I said, pointing to a cover photo of some hunky guy wearing little more than a police whistle and six-pack abs, "why do you have all these magazines?"

"Oh, didn't I tell you?" Jeff hesitated, finishing off his drink. "I'm gay," he said casually.

It seems hard to imagine now, but until that moment I didn't have a clue. This was a time after all, when mainstream America still thought of Rock Hudson as a ladies' man. The word "faggot" popped into my head. Guys at school called other guys this all the time; it was an accepted slur, a catch-all insult. Jeff is a faggot, I thought. My best friend is a faggot. "Well?" Jeff prompted. "What are you thinking?" He watched me from across the room.

How was I supposed to feel about this revelation? Betrayed? Angry? Grossed out? What little I had heard or read about gay people, these seemed to be the usual reactions. Come to think of it, these were the same type of reactions Michael anticipated from his co-workers at the Big Q, even though, supposedly, times have changed.

"Oh, didn't I tell you?" In lieu of a real answer, I simply mimicked Jeff's words, struck by how casually he had announced he was gay. Later, this line would become part of our standard comic repertoire whenever we caught up on big life events. ("Oh, didn't I tell you? I got married." "Oh, didn't I tell you? I had another baby.") At that moment, however, I just didn't know what else to say.

"Hmm . . ." I pretended to be searching my memory, "I guess you forget to mention you were gay *these past three years.*"

Jeff laughed, obviously relieved. "I knew you'd be okay with this," he crossed the room and gave me a hug. Apparently, Jeff had heard acceptance in my response, whether it was there or not. Looking back at that time, I think I was too young or too distracted by my own insecurities to recognize my strengths or my prejudices. Maybe that's why I craved Jeff's friendship so much, and why I still love him to this day. Jeff always said I was the funniest girl he knew, and so I was funny. After he told me he was gay, he assumed I was a decent human being, and so I decided to act like one.

That night and many more nights, Jeff and I went dancing at Heaven, which, if memory serves, looks pretty much the same as Babylon, the gay club where Michael and Brian and Ted and Emmett hang out and dance, among other more provocative behaviors.

When Jeff and I talked on the phone a few weeks ago, he complained about his paunch, and told me he dyes his chest hair with Clairol. I suggested Natural Match—that's what I sometimes use on my grey roots—but he preferred Clairol because one pack lasted him at least three dye jobs. Jeff seemed more wistful than usual during our conversation, talking about our careers and how we'd succeeded, more or less, at making a living as writers and editors. He also told me he was planning a trip to San Francisco for his upcoming fiftieth birthday.

What Jeff didn't tell me the last time we spoke was that his partner of two decades had recently broken up with him. He also failed to mention that he was drinking too much, and feeling depressed. "Oh, didn't I tell you?" I can almost hear him saying in that same casual tone he used thirty years ago to let me know he was gay. "I'm going to kill myself, so this is goodbye."

Of course, Jeff didn't say this, at least not to me.

But that's okay, I tell myself, and pop in another *Queer as Folk*. Because when I watch the show I'm reminded that Teddy hid his crystal meth addiction from Emmett, his lover at the time, but Emmett still forgave him. And when Brian was first diagnosed with testicular cancer, he didn't even tell Michael, who would have wanted to help him through it, but it didn't matter anyway because a few episodes later they were back on the dance floor, as close as ever. And when Michael's uncle Vic, a self-proclaimed "Old Queen" with HIV, was killed off in season four, he still appeared in the show from time to time in flashbacks and dream sequences, looking happier and healthier than ever.

But that's the beauty of TV, and cable to boot, where anything is possible, and you can always bring people back by replaying earlier episodes.

A VERMONTY STATE OF MIND

I should have known that Vermont and I would be a peculiar fit the first night I arrived over fifteen years ago. My husband Steve and I had moved here so that he could go to graduate school and I could be a "spouse." Because our university housing wasn't available the day we arrived in town, we splurged on a room at a bed and breakfast advertised as having "a cozy atmosphere and charming décor." After all, if we were going to live here (just for a few years, or so we thought at the time) we might as well immerse ourselves in the Vermont experience. And what was more Vermonty than a bed and breakfast?

The colonial-style inn was indeed a charming B&B, but having never stayed in one before, I'd gotten caught up in the romance, rather than the reality of what this actually meant. While I had envisioned a Marriott that smelled of scones, this inn was actually an extension of somebody's home. The owners, Brenda and Wayne, were youngish retirees clearly devoted to two things: amassing collectibles, and lavishing attention on their guests.

But here is the thing. I hate collectibles, which might as well be called breakables, given my heavy caffeine consumption. Yet here I was surrounded by hundreds of them. Glass figurines. Porcelain dolls. Herds of miniature carved elephants roaming the fireplace mantle and antique end tables. What's more, when I travel I like to be anonymous, or at least not feel guilted into looking at my hosts' photo albums of their nature walks through Northern New England, as they (and their elephants) hover nearby.

This first (and last) B&B experience should have raised a giant red flag—leave Vermont and live someplace else, someplace less "cozy" with three-star motels owned by impersonal corpglomerations, where you can toss your cheap bottle of wine and *People* magazine in the bedroom trash and not feel ridiculously self conscious.

Still, all these years later, I find myself settled in the Green Mountain State, having bought a house here after my husband finished his dissertation and received a good job offer. Over the years, I have come to appreciate Vermont— its natural beauty, its quiet smugness over all those other states that legalized billboards. Yet once in a while I am reminded of my misfit status.

A few Saturdays ago, I was visiting my friend Ellen who lives in a neighboring town. En route to her house, I saw a pick-up truck with a bumper sticker reading, *Don't New Jersey Vermont.* I am not from New Jersey, but having grown up just a few hours from there, I have spent enough time enjoying its over-crowded shores, and later playing the slots in its smoke-filled casinos, to want a little more of that action.

"Do *you* ever feel like an outsider in Vermont?" I asked Ellen as she fixed us one of her special, healing herbal teas in the sunny kitchen of her restored farmhouse.

"No," she answered, which didn't come as any surprise. Like me, Ellen was a city transplant, only unlike me she had taken to all things Vermont with the zeal of a convert. Once a Type A executive, she now enjoyed contra dancing, wore all-natural deodorant, and had become a committed locavore, a term defined as "a person who eats only food grown and produced close to home," but that always makes me think of vampires.

"Do you feel like an outsider?" Ellen asked, setting a plate of fresh-baked strawberry muffins on the table.

"It's just that sometimes I don't feel Vermonty enough to live here," I explained. "It's like one of these days I'm going to be found out and asked to leave to make room for a real Vermonter; someone who has fortitude and who gets excited about raising chickens."

"Don't be silly," Ellen countered. "All kinds of people live in Vermont." She took a sip of tea, prompting me to do the same, but there were flecks floating in the liquid and it smelled funny, like a urinary tract infection. Why couldn't Ellen just settle for normal, *un*healing tea, I thought meanly. "I have the opposite of a green thumb," I announced, noting the vase of lovely flowers on Ellen's kitchen windowsill, plucked from her lovingly-tended garden. "Vermonters are like one big, happy garden club, to which I don't belong."

Ellen laughed. "No one is going to kick you out of the state just because you kill houseplants."

"I also can't ski," I argued. "Plus I'm thin-blooded, which means I'm always cold, and spend at least five months out of the year here wrapped in one of those fleece body bags, with a wad of damp Kleenex tucked in my sleeve."

"I don't ski either," Ellen reminded me.

"No, but you snowshoe," I helped myself to a second muffin. Naturally, Ellen had picked the strawberries herself. "Plus you're good at baking and you're crafty, both of which are completely Vermonty. I tried to knit a scarf once," I added, "and the whole time I was slaving away on the stupid thing, all I could think of was, *Why not just go to K-Mart and buy a better-looking one for fifteen bucks.*"

"You're missing the bigger picture." Ellen retrieved her latest knitting project from a tote and began clicking her needles. "Being Vermonty isn't just about what you can or can't do. It's more a state of mind," she explained.

Huh?

Before I left Ellen's house, she insisted I take some leaf lettuce from her vegetable garden. Normally, I eat lettuce from California that is triple washed, then sealed in an air-tight bag. This fresh-picked stuff would take tedious rinsing to rid it of whatever bugs thrived in organic conditions. Still, I appreciated the freebie, and set the clump of frilly greens on the passenger seat. At the least, I thought, I could use it to ward off locavores.

The drive home was pretty—trees in mid-summer bloom, and picture postcard scenes of grazing farm animals and country towns. As I drove, I mulled over Ellen's comment—*Vermont is a state of mind.* I didn't exactly know what she meant by this; Ellen and I had been friends for years, but we often spoke different languages. Still, the more I thought about her words, the better I felt.

About twenty minutes later, I turned down Route 14, which runs parallel to the White River and intersects with my road. I followed the familiar path of the water, admiring, as always, the river's curves and sparkling beauty. No, I wasn't Vermonty, I concluded, and likely never would be, given the fact that I would rather raise the dead than chickens. But despite this reality, Vermont still felt like home, and I knew that I didn't want to leave here.

THE REST HOME

People say youth is wasted on the young. I don't know about that, but I do think nursing homes are wasted on the old. What I wouldn't give to move into my dad's skilled nursing facility, a lap of luxury known as Garden Spot.

I am sitting with my dad in his private room, demarcated from the other residents' rooms with a wooden door decoration that reads, *Be Nice to Your Kids, They Choose Your Nursing Home.* Of course, here, "private" is more loosely defined, given that doors, including bathroom doors, are usually left open as aides come and go, cheerfully asking about bowel movements.

In my real life (over four-hundred miles away from Garden Spot), I have been married for more than two decades and not once left the bathroom door open for my husband to see me on the toilet. If he's in the next room, I run the faucet so he can't hear me peeing. Who am I trying to kid? This is the man who stood at the foot of the bed when I gave birth to our two daughters.

But at Garden Spot all pretense is gone. Most of the residents wear diapers and terry cloth bibs referred to as clothing protectors. On a regular basis, any one of them is likely to let out a string of curses at a visiting family member, weep uncontrollably, ramble on about some ancient wrong, or idly diddle themselves while shuffling down the hallway. I am a married mother of two children. Yet all of these behaviors I could easily imagine myself doing countless times throughout the day, save for my tenuous hold on decorum. Oh, to be able to simply let go.

My dad's room is furnished with a single bed with rails. His comfy, overstuffed recliner has automatic controls that ease him not only backward but forward, so that the aides don't have to strain their backs during transfers. Happy things are everywhere—a clock with postage-stamp sized pictures of family members designating each hour, a tin watering can bursting with silk sunflowers, and a top dresser drawer stocked with Hershey Kisses and Cup O' Soups for visitors, amid the support socks to prevent blood clots. At Garden Spot, you may be old and infirm, but you never have to worry about Death catching you unprepared.

My dad, who lives here because he suffered a massive stroke, dozes in his recliner while he receives his breathing treatment through a plastic mask propped over his nose and mouth. When the respiratory therapist first arrived at my dad's room this morning, I asked him if I could have a breathing treatment, too, but he acted like I was kidding. The apparatus makes a soft, pleasant hiss, and I imagine the treatment is like getting a hit at one of those oxygen bars that were trendy a couple years ago, or maybe still trendy for all I know. I've always wanted to go to one of those bars, but I live in Vermont, where the oxygen is outside and most people aren't willing to package it for you. If you want to breathe where I live, you're on your own.

I relax in my dad's wheelchair watching a *Murder, She Wrote* rerun on the television. The main character, Jessica Fletcher, is a sixty-something mystery author who lives in a small coastal village in Cabot Cove, Maine, and happens to stumble upon a murder once a week. Jessica doesn't know how to drive, but she gets around plenty with just her bicycle.

Wouldn't I love Jessica's two-wheeling lifestyle? I think. It seems like I spend half my life in a car, carting one kid or another here or there, despite the fact that I hate to drive and that I'm not very good at it. My tendency is to either speed or crawl; my emotions constantly flip-flop from road rage at all the other drivers as incompetent as me, and sudden panic at the notion that this is just one more way I could die a violent death. Worse yet, I'm constantly aware of the possibility of involving my daughters in an accident en route to their piano lessons or basketball practices or jewelry-making workshops, thus cutting short their over-scheduled young lives, not to mention making them late once again.

Murder, She Wrote ends and is followed by another *Murder, She Wrote*. In this episode, Jessica's niece (Jessica herself is a widow and childless) is accused of doing away with an old boyfriend, and needs her aunt's help in finding the true killer. During a commercial, I flip to the television listings on the Guide Channel, and discover that the station is airing a *Murder, She Wrote* marathon! Twenty-four hours of *Murder, She Wrote!*

You cannot imagine my happiness. Given the long-running popularity of the show, I have years and years of *Murder, She Wrote* to catch up on. Years I was distracted after college by random jobs (loan collections, bartending, copywriting), then trying to land a husband, then going to graduate school, then more attempts to start, or at least find, a fulfilling career as a writer, then having babies, then juggling work and motherhood and essentially multitasking but somehow underachieving my way through years and years of life, while never catching up on all the things I have to do, or should be doing, or would rather be doing, such as watching back-to-back episodes of murder in a charming small town in Maine.

Stacey, one of the aides I met during my last visit to Garden Spot a few months ago, pops into my dad's room to check on him. "You're Myles' youngest daughter!" she announces with enthusiasm. Like most members of the nursing home staff, Stacey makes me feel special for no other reason than just showing up. If only the people in my real life—my family, my friends, the editors I work with— shared these minimal requirements for appreciation. Stacey removes my dad's breathing mask and perches his glasses on his nose, even though his stroke rendered him virtually blind.

"Aren't you the writer from Vermont?" she asks me.

I lower the volume of the TV and shake myself out of my *Murder, She Wrote* stupor. Yes, I nod, I am indeed the writer from Vermont, though it has never occurred to me to frame my life in such romantic-sounding terms. I picture myself at work, not at my desk that overlooks the trash on the back porch, but cozily curled up in a hand-hewn rocker by a roaring fire, penning Frost-like thoughts in a cloth-bound journal.

"Myles, hon?" Stacey interrupts my fantasizing, and adjusts my dad's fleece blanket with the image of a howling wolf. One of the volunteers at Garden Spot gave it to him, and it is the only blanket that seems to keep him warm. "Do you need me to take you to the bathroom?"

At noon, I wheel my dad to lunch in one of Garden Spot's spacious dining rooms. En route, I hear a woman's feeble voice call out, "Help me. Help me. Help me." When we pass her room, I peek inside. She is sitting up in bed, her white hair as wispy as the contents of a milk pod. Her eyes stare vacantly at the wall, and she clutches a baby doll under her chin. "*Help me. Help me. Help me,*" she repeats tonelessly, patting her baby doll's back. The chanting and patting seem to soothe her.

I once skimmed an article in a doctor's waiting room, advising readers to come up with a mantra to help them meditate or simply do nothing. Who has time to do nothing? I thought with resentment, but now I knew the answer.

If I lived in Garden Spot, I would have a mantra. And I'd bring my favorite doll from childhood. Her name was Baby Drowsy and she wore pink, polka dot pajamas. Baby Drowsy was soft and squishy and always made me feel better, even when everyone else in the world was mean to me.

My dad and I arrive at the dining room, resplendent with planters of fall mums and miniature pumpkins adorning each tabletop. The seasonal decorations remind me that I forgot to take my daughters shopping for their Halloween costumes, which will be less than a week away by the time I return to Vermont. This means that they will once again have to choose from K-Mart's decimated racks, reduced to a mish mash of Disney's least popular characters, gory masks with no strings, and molting feather boas. I also remember that I forgot to return the girls' school picture forms, which are likely buried amid the stack of unpaid bills, expired coupons, and flyers for swing dance lessons that I have been collecting off and on for decades.

Muzak plays quietly in the dining room. My father sits at his reserved table for four, joined by Agnes, who is beautifully dressed but skeletal, and her husband, Michael, who looks relatively robust with his shock of steel-grey hair and raptor-like, black eyes. Another resident, Walter, is missing, though a table-top placard with his dietary restrictions—no liquids, no dairy—holds his place. At Garden Spot, there is no pressure to make small talk, or even stay awake for that matter. Agnes dozes in her wheelchair, while Michael concentrates on navigating his unsteady fork to his mouth.

So much food! And none of it prepared by me. Ham steak today (solid or ground), mashed potatoes, fluffy white rolls and butter pats, broccoli, carrots, fruit cup, milk with or without thickener, and coffee. And for dessert: white-frosted cake with sprinkles, or a non-dairy ice cream treat.

At home, meal preparation—breakfasts, packed lunches, dinners, breakfasts, packed lunches, dinners—feels never-ending. It is also made worse by the fact that the school guidance counselor persists on sending home handouts about the benefits of the family meal, reportedly a cure-all for everything from poor grades to teenage pregnancy.

The problem, however, is that no one in my family will eat the same thing. So most of our family meals are frozen dinners. We sit down together at the table. The microwave beeps. It's time to stir someone's Stouffers Swedish Meatballs and reheat for three minutes. We sit down again. The microwave beeps. Someone else's macaroni and cheese is still frozen in the middle, or their Boca Burger is overcooked on the edges. How in the world does my daughter's guidance counselor expect me to prevent teenage pregnancy when microwave cooking times are so uneven?

My dad declares that he is full after I feed him his ground ham and fruit cup. I know the dietary consultants here assess the food left on every resident's plate, in order to make sure they are taking in enough calories. But what harm, I think, in eating my dad's cake with sprinkles? Like a luxury cruise, the food at Garden Spot is included in the package price, so why should it go to waste?

After I wheel my father back to his room, another aide, Tony, appears to help him settle in for his afternoon nap, leaving me to take a leisurely stroll through the facility. Gone is my usual "Impatient Mommy" speed-walk, typically with one arm extended backward toward a trailing kid. I know just what I look like as Impatient Mommy because my daughters have learned to mimic me to perfection. At home, I am always in a hurry, rushing from somewhere to somewhere else, consistently seventeen minutes late. But at Garden Spot, I am free to lollygag. Why hurry, after all, when the days here go on and on, defined only by mealtimes and medications?

I stroll past residents' rooms, reading the nameplates along the way—Cora, Earl, Verna, Ruth, Grace. Despite my own encroaching menopause, the old-fashioned names make me feel young, even youthful again, like somebody's granddaughter, or great granddaughter.

Eventually, I exit the automatic doors of the skilled nursing unit and enter the carpeted thoroughfare of Garden Spot's assisted living facility. The "Jolly Trolley" putters around me in the wide hallway, tooting its horn in a friendly heads up. Its driver stops a few yards ahead to allow a stooped man in plaid golf pants to hobble aboard. The Jolly Trolley is even better than Jessica Fletcher's bicycle, I think. You don't even have to pedal.

Here, everything you could possibly want or need is within comfortable walking or wheeling distance: an information desk with free coffee; a beauty parlor; a computer center; a lending library; a Gift Shoppe; an elegant gathering room with a grand piano and fancy coffee table books on subjects from Dolly Parton to Victorian tea services.

Near the entrance to the solarium (home to thriving exotic plants, two caged cockatiels, and a fountain with cherubs) is a floor-to-ceiling aquarium built right into the wall. Inside the tank is a small man in a wet suit who is polishing the interior of the glass. I finger wave a hello, wishing a small man in a wet suit would come to my house to clean. At Garden Spot, everything is kept sparkly bright. I could happily live in any one of the ladies' restrooms, which are tastefully appointed, and regularly deodorized with automated puffs of floral air freshener. And in every stall, an emergency pull cord!

When I return to my dad's room in the skilled nursing unit, he is again reclined in his comfy chair, covered, as usual, in his fleece wolf blanket. His eyes are closed.

Murder, She Wrote is still on the television, but the volume is set on low. "Daddy," I whisper, "Are you awake?" He doesn't answer, but his breathing is even.

I decide to catch up on some work. In fact, I have brought my laptop with me to Garden Spot for this very reason. The writer from Vermont, after all, has deadlines and professional obligations. I settle into my dad's wheelchair and open a blank document. Maybe I will start by writing something new.

The room is warm; the thermostat is set in the high seventies to accommodate my dad's poor circulation. I stare at the blank computer screen and my own reflection stares back at me, older than I imagined. In my mind, I see myself as a tired twenty-something, but the creases from my nose to my mouth remind me otherwise. I am getting old. I don't have a real job with benefits or a pension. I don't know which haircut is right for my face shape. I am equally self-centered and insecure, and my daughters will have to go trick-or-treating in gory, age-inappropriate masks with makeshift strings.

"What should I write about?" I ask my dad. The writer from Vermont is overwhelmed.

"Big plans for your escape," he responds. Since his stroke, my dad's consciousness drifts from sleep to wakefulness, from befuddlement to lucidity. He has been like this for years, but it still gets to me, these moments when his mind resurfaces, reminding me of the father he used to be.

"Are you planning your escape?" I ask. The mid-sun cuts through the window beside his recliner, illuminating his skull beneath his sunken cheeks, and his yellow, nursing home pallor. He doesn't answer. That quickly, he has drifted back to sleep, or to somewhere else. I shut down my computer and wheel myself closer to my dad's recliner. Even through his heavy wolf blanket, I can feel his bony wrist, the looseness of his skin.

Help me. Help me. Help me, I think, patting my dad's useless left arm. At Garden Spot, I have time to meditate, or simply do nothing. *Help me. Help me. Help me.*

This is a rest home. I close my eyes. Here I have permission to rest.

THE BOY OF SUMMER

The summer before my junior year of high school, I divided
my time between working the counter at Willie's Meat Store
and hanging out at Skyline Swimming Pool. At the meat
store, my boss kept the calf livers in a bucket in the walk-in
cooler. Thirty years later, I can still bring back the sensation of reaching into that cold, wet pile, groping through
the organs, feeling the heft of each liver in my open palm.
Maybe because I was sixteen at the time, in the throes of
some stage of sensual development, that experience felt a lot
more pleasurable than it probably sounds here.

Equally enduring from that summer was another sensual
memory, this one involving me and my teenage heartthrob,
Dale Zug, at Skyline Pool. The entire interaction between us
lasted only thirty or forty seconds, but that was plenty of time
for it to become imprinted on my brain, specifically on the
part where certain physical encounters, however fleeting,
are processed and re-imagined as soft-core pornography in
my head.

Dale Zug was a year older than I, new to our high school
in Lancaster, Pennsylvania, from some place with Southern
accents as warm as pulled taffy. I remember him as lean and
easy-going in his Levis 501 jeans. Like all heartthrobs from the
'70s, he wore his dark hair longish and parted far to the side,
with a sweep of bangs across his forehead. He wasn't among
the most popular boys at our school, not a jock or the life of
the party. He struck me as deep, but not brooding; different,

but not weird. He had a great smile. A really great smile.

Dale Zug and I never had a conversation; it's unlikely he even knew my name. Sometimes our paths would cross accidentally, but more often I simply tried to be where I thought he would show up. This would have been a lot easier if I'd had any musical or acting talent because Dale Zug sang in the choir, and had a small part in the school play. Even these extra-curricular activities fed my attraction, offering more evidence of an artistic soul.

Here, I should disclose that, for the sake of discretion, I have invented the name Dale Zug, though I have tried to assign him a fake name with a comparable quirkiness. This too contributed to the real Dale Zug's charm, the way his first name and odd last name created an intriguing dynamic. To me, he was never just Dale. Always Dale Zug.

"Don't you think Dale Zug is the cutest?" I asked my friend Patty whenever she and I talked about boys, which was pretty much all the time. Patty was the only person I eventually confided in about my secret crush, and one of my few friends from high school with whom I have kept in touch. In fact, the last time I asked Patty this question we were in our forties. I was staying at her house after doing a book event near her town, and we were looking through our high school yearbook, gabbing about old times.

"I guess he's all right looking," Patty said dismissively. In his senior photo, Dale Zug wore an Irish Fisherman's sweater with a tie. Granted, this wasn't his best look, but seeing that sweep of dark wavy hair still made me sigh with romantic longing. Patty's lack of enthusiasm about Dale Zug's cuteness did nothing to deter my own. Her judgment had long been suspect ever since she revealed her own teenage crush on John Davidson, an entertainer whose renowned dimples did nothing for me.

"John Davidson," I'd scoff whenever Patty brought him up. "Why don't you just make out with a baby's bottom?"

The summer I worked at Willie's Meat Store, I was the youngest and hence lowliest employee, so my boss scheduled me to work the hours no one else wanted, mostly evenings and weekends. That was fine by me because I needed to keep my weekdays free. It was important I hang out at Skyline Pool to do the following:

Watch and wait for Dale Zug.

Fry myself in baby oil.

Force myself into the pool inch by inch because I didn't like the shock of cold water.

Avoid the deep end because I couldn't swim. Comb my long, wet hair.

Comb my friends' long, wet hair.

Play Bloody Knuckles, a card game that is as violent as it sounds.

Feel self conscious about my body in my blue-striped bikini.

Now when I look at photographs of myself at age sixteen, I can see my size and shape were well within the normal range, with certain body parts even showing some signs of promise. That said, if you went by the recurring comments from some of my friends' mothers, you would think I was the stilt-walker at the fair.

"Just look at those long legs!" Mrs. Herr, in her skirted bathing suit, seemed compelled to greet me every time I encountered her at the pool.

"They just go on and on and on," round Mrs. Dorfmann concurred, observing my great height from her low-slung beach chair.

There was this to be endured, and then there was my own unfortunate habit of measuring my looks against those of Dale Zug's girlfriend, a dancer I'll refer to as Thumbelina.

As the name implies, Thumbelina was petite, which is not to say underdeveloped, with glossy blond hair that turned up at the tips, and pretty, delicate features. In comparison, with my disproportionately long legs and a face still padded with baby fat, I felt like a colt with the mumps.

At Skyline, as in school, certain social protocols prevailed, meaning everyone knew the expanse of lawn to the right of the snack bar was the equivalent of the cool kids' table in the cafeteria. On this section of grass, the popular girls spread out their towels, thus marking the center of our teenage universe, around which the other girls orbited in order of popularity. In the solar system that was my high school, the placement of my towel indicated that I was the equivalent of Uranus, a word I still have trouble saying without embarrassment.

All this is to say that for me, going to Skyline Pool was sometimes fun, but more accurately a labor of love. I went every chance I got because Dale Zug showed up with just enough frequency to keep hope alive. It was a thrill to watch him saunter across the grass, his broad, bony shoulders tapering down to a pair of baggy, turquoise swim trunks.

This was not one of those much-anticipated Dale Zug days, or so I thought when a bunch of us decided to play Nerf Keep-Away in the pool, boys against girls. The game was simple. You tossed the Nerf to one of your teammates, and tried not to let anyone from the other team intercept it. Basically, the game was an excuse for the boyfriends to get physical with their girlfriends, all under the guise of Nerf fun. Because I didn't have a boyfriend, most of my time was spent standing in the shallow end, yelling, "I'm open, I'm open," while waving my arms like a shipwreck survivor.

The sun was out in full force that day, creating a sharp glare across the water's surface. I had to visor my eyes with my hand to follow the Nerf action. My friend Cathy had the ball, but a boy named Doug, whom everybody called Zit, was fast approaching her.

"I'm open, I'm open!" I yelled.

Cathy tossed me the Nerf—a bad throw, wide and high—but with those long legs of mine I catapulted out of the water, arm raised toward the sky. Thwack. I caught it!

Before I had even landed, Dale Zug was behind me, squeezing me tight around my middle. I twisted, still holding the Nerf over my head. The front of our bodies connected, hip bone to hip bone. He jumped, grabbed for the ball, missed. He tickled my sides. We wrestled. He picked me up by my waist, lifting me out of the water. Dale Zug was strong. Oh my God! *Dale Zug was strong and could sing!*

Then he dunked me and tugged the Nerf from my clenched fist. I had never wanted to hold onto something more tightly in my whole life.

Fast-forward thirty years. By now, maybe because my attraction to Dale Zug had formed mostly from adolescent hormones and romantic fantasies, he lingered in my memory more as an ideal than a real person. Dale Zug, my teenage heartthrob; Dale Zug, my sexy boy of summer. While I never saw him again after graduation, at least, I thought, we would always have Skyline.

Over the years, my imagination has replayed that encounter in the pool many times, except with a different ending.

Dale Zug and I exchange a heated glance, the Nerf ball long forgotten. Water drops sparkle off his cheekbones. He hooks a finger into the band of my bikini bottoms, drawing me to him. Our hip bones meet, then our lips. He reaches behind my neck and slowly, teasingly, releases the bow to my bathing suit top. I put my arms around him, feeling the muscles in his back.

My fingers begin to trace the waistband of his turquoise swim trunks . . .

Considering how much Dale Zug meant to me in high school and beyond, it was only natural that the first thing I did after I joined Facebook was to try and find him. At first, my searches yielded no matches, but every so often I'd try again, and then one day—Dale Zug! I clicked on his name. The page showed no photo, and revealed only one bit of information: Texas was listed as his current home.

My pulse picked up, just like it used to when I imagined myself talking to him in high school. This had to be him, I thought. How many Dale Zugs could there be? Plus, a Texas address made sense. I recalled the thrill of hearing those slow Southern syllables as he recited his few lines in the high school play.

But should I send Dale Zug a request to be friends on Facebook? Now that I had found him, I wasn't sure what to do. What if he didn't remember me from school? Would he assume I was some kind of weirdo stalker? Or, what if he did remember me? Then he might really think I was some kind of weirdo stalker, since that pretty much fit my profile back then.

Back and forth the debate went in my head: Did he know I used to have a crush on him? But he couldn't have known, not unless that Patty blabbed. But would she blab? Maybe not to Dale Zug *directly*, but what about to one of his friends?—until eventually I asked myself, *What am I, in tenth grade again?* Instead of answering, I quickly clicked send.

The next day, Dale Zug approved my request to be his friend! He even wrote me a short message. "Joni, Nice to hear from you." Oh, what I would have given to hear him say those words to me in high school! (Yes, I'm talking about my virginity.) I wrote back to confirm that he was, indeed, the right Dale Zug and not by some eponymous fluke a different one. In his response he explained that his family had moved to Pennsylvania when he was in high school, but Texas had always been home.

Not wanting to seem pushy, I didn't write back. I also needed time to process this new reality. Dale Zug and I were friends, or at least Facebook friends. This had to count for something, but what?

By the time Dale Zug posted a photograph of himself online, I'd already had the experience of seeing other high school classmates age thirty years overnight. Or so it seemed, given my mental image of most of these people remained frozen in the late '70s. I clicked on the Facebook page of my former high school friend Susan, for example, expecting to see her as she appeared in our old field hockey team picture. Instead her father's face loomed back at me, or at least his heavy jowls. When I found our homecoming queen, a pretty Mennonite girl, her profile picture looked remarkably similar to the church lady. How had this happened? *When* had this happened?

Still, it wasn't the fact that my lean, teenage Dale Zug had been replaced by a much beefier, middle-aged man that shocked me so much as the fact that, in his Facebook photo, Dale Zug was chomping on a cigar, holding up a hooked fish, and putting the squeeze on a fifty-something gal showing Texas-sized cleavage. I don't care how much time changes us all, Thumbelina this woman was not. Dale Zug had captioned the photo: *Me and my Baby!*

Baby? What kind of grown man publicly refers to his spouse or significant other as baby? The options were depressingly obvious: cigar-chomping Texans, men on their fourth marriage, and any male the opposite of appealing to me. Within a short time, Dale Zug became one of my most active Facebook friends, intermingling daily updates about his life with political commentary. He described himself as right wing and conservative. He was a diehard Cowboys fan. He loved to cook and fish and golf. He cited a deep and passionate love for God. He asked people to pray for his "Daddy" who was going in for surgery. He denounced the president and all those "lunatic liberals" who were trying to take away his freedoms.

"Finally!" Dale Zug enthused in one post, "Got my concealed handgun license in the mail yesterday! Dale is armed. Don't tread on me. Come and try to get it NObama!" Reading his Facebook entries, inundated with a bring-it-on mentality and atrocious misspellings, it quickly became clear that if I had met Dale Zug as an adult, I never would have sought out his company, let alone built a fantasy life around him. For one thing, I was one of those lunatic liberals he was constantly railing against, though I prefer to think of myself as a liberal Democrat who believes in strict gun control. In contrast, if Glenn Beck, Sarah Palin, Rush Limbaugh, and Ann Coulter had an unprotected orgy, their resulting spawn would be Dale Zug's long list of Facebook "likes"—the Tea Party Patriots, The Heritage Foundation, Fox News, Anything about Guns . . .

Still, I was glad I had found him after all these years. Dale Zug and I had a history, even if he didn't know it. Call it nostalgia or sentimentality, but I wanted us to be friends. Plus, it felt like something bigger was at stake. Several years ago, a friend of mine who is a professor had described me as a hybrid of Red and Blue America. While this was putting way too much stock in the fact that I listen to country music, I liked this vision of myself, as someone who could transcend the rancor polarizing our country.

Meanwhile, Dale Zug continued to barrage his social network with more news of government wrong-doing and impending disaster: Obama sells billions of dollars worth of arms to

Muslim terrorists! Illegal immigrants create leprosy epidemic! Liberals put America on the brink of collapse!

About the only issue Dale Zug wasn't alarmist about was global warming. "A freaking hoax," he called it.

Yet, despite our opposing views, a part of me had to hand it to him: he wasn't afraid to wear his beliefs on his red, white, and blue sleeve. This touched a nerve. Not only am I not politically active, I actually feel embarrassed for that same group of five or six protestors I drive by every morning, waving their hand-painted signs at commuters. I want to stop the war, too, but not if it looks that pathetic.

Maybe it was Dale Zug's influence, or simply that Facebook makes it easy to register your opinion, but one day I decided to click on a checkbox to show my support for healthcare reform. At this point, the reform bill had already become law, but Republicans had been ratcheting up their threats to have it repealed. It felt good to make this small, public gesture, to give voice to my beliefs.

"Are you a Communist?" Dale Zug responded almost immediately on my Facebook wall.

"Say what?!" I wrote back. Except for our brief initial exchange, this was the first personal message he had sent me. "Be afraid," he warned. "Be very afraid of government death panels."

Let it go, I told myself. For one thing, trying to have a meaningful political back and forth through those little comments boxes was exhausting, not to mention the fact that those idiotic, nonexistent death panels didn't even dignify a response.

"Let's just agree to disagree," I wrote back, trying to maintain my equanimity. I could feel something slipping away, call it my patience, or hope, but I just couldn't, I wouldn't, let political differences come between me and my teenage heartthrob.

Months passed, and each time Dale Zug let loose with another burst of moral outrage, I had to steel myself to read it. But to not read his comments felt wrong, like sticking my fingers in my ears and chanting la-la-la just because someone was saying something I didn't want to hear.

Call it cowardice or a lack of conviction, but I never countered any of his opinions with my own, not after his crack about me being a Communist. For all Dale Zug knew, I seconded his views. You're damn right mosques don't belong in America! Hell no, I won't press one for English! And all you folks on the dole, if you can afford alcohol and cigarettes, you sure as hell don't need food stamps!

In contrast, Dale Zug had no problem confronting me when I ventured an opinion or acknowledged an interest he didn't like.

When I became a fan of the White House, for example, he felt compelled to set the record straight. "O.B.A.M.A.," he wrote, "One Big Ass Mistake America."

When I became an online supporter of National Public Radio, he called the organization elitist. "What makes any of you so dam [sic] smart?" (As always, I was tempted to call him on his misspellings, until it struck me that this was what he was referring to when he labeled me elitist.)

Because most of my other Facebook friends were liberal Vermonters and writer-types like me, or at least not right-wing extremists, this made his comments stand out all the more. Amid all the excited chatter about the BBC book challenge and how to decrease your carbon footprint, a shout-out to the Liberal Nut Company was bound to get noticed.

"Who is this guy?" several of my friends asked me, clearly surprised to see someone like Dale Zug in my social network. Sometimes they took it upon themselves to respond directly to his right-wing outbursts, occasionally in measured tones, just as often with equal vitriol.

More than one person suggested I unfriend him.

Usually, I have no problem unfriending people on Facebook — the cousin who sent me one too many quizzes, the author whose status updates never failed to mention her new book, the father who thought every sentence out of his kid's mouth was worthy of an Art Linkletter special. But if Dale Zug and I couldn't be Facebook friends, I worried, what hope was there for the rest of a divided country?

Besides, I reminded myself, politics were just one aspect of the man. Thanks to Facebook, I had plenty of other windows to peek into his life. He posted pictures of Texas wildflowers. He advocated for local charities. He shared his favorite recipe for green-bean casserole. I liked green-bean casserole, sort of. So why should it matter that he was stockpiling weapons, or that one of his photo albums showcased his 38 Special, 9mm Kahr, and Glock 32? Here was a family man with a generous heart. In one post he gushed, "Just bought my baby a new shotgun for her birthday!"

And so our Facebook friendship continued, until one day I noted my support of the Coffee Party, a grass roots movement formed to counter the Tea Party, and to promote cooperation in government. Even as I agreed to the group's pledge to conduct myself in a way that was civil, honest, and respectful toward people with whom I disagreed, I knew this one gesture would probably be the extent of my involvement.

As I should have predicted, Dale Zug sounded in all too soon. He wrote on my wall that the Coffee Party was nothing but a bunch of pathetic progressives. "If all you brainwashed, Birkenstock-wearing . . ." his message continued, but that was it. I didn't even finish reading his sentence. In a spike of anger, I went to Dale Zug's Facebook page and removed him from my friends. With one click, I took a stand. With a second click, I confirmed, *Yes, I was sure I wanted him gone.*

He was an asshole! An idiot! For over a year, I had put up with his stupid rants against the government. When he questioned my intelligence, and trashed my beliefs, I told myself not to take it personally, to try and understand his point of view. But this time he had gone too far.

Birkenstocks! I would never, ever be caught dead wearing Birkenstocks, no matter how popular they were in Vermont, or any other blue or red state in the country. Those tire tread soles, those hideous cork foot-beds, those thick buckled straps. How could anyone look at those straps and not think of in-patient restraints? Dale Zug had gotten away with calling me many names since we had become Facebook friends, but he crossed the line when he presumed to put shoes on my feet.

At first it was a relief to open my Facebook page and experience a relative peace and quiet. I didn't miss for one second Dale Zug's apocalyptic warnings about Mexican murderers taking over the good old U.S. of A., his battle cries to restore America's traditional moral principles, or his links to Sarah Palin's Alaska.

Yet, over time, other emotions unsettled me. First, there was a niggling of shame. For months, I had remained silent as Dale Zug espoused views that resounded with hate, intolerance, and racism. Yet, only when he challenged my fashion sense, only when his mudslinging splattered onto my vanity, did I bother to do anything about it. I was an activist, all right, at least when it came to foot-wear.

And then there was the image of myself as the common ground between Red and Blue America. My one small effort to promulgate civil discourse had left me feeling bruised, purple. In the end, just like Dale Zug and all those other people I blame for the animosity within our country, I had responded to our political differences with knee-jerk anger and name-calling.

But my illusion of tolerance wasn't the only fantasy I lost.

Months have passed since I unfriended Dale Zug. I know now that my teenage heartthrob is long gone, and probably never even existed, at least not in the way I had imagined him. Still, old habits die hard, especially when it comes to matters of the heart. Sometimes, I close my eyes, and there we are again on that hot, sunny day, back in the water at Skyline Pool.

Dale Zug and I exchange a heated glance, the Nerf ball long forgotten. Water drops sparkle off his cheekbones. He hooks a finger into the band of my bikini bottoms, drawing me closer. Our hip bones meet, then our lips. He reaches behind my neck and slowly, teasingly, releases the bow to my bathing suit top.

I put my arms around him, feeling the muscles in his back. My fingers begin to trace the waistband of his turquoise swim trunks . . .

And that's when I feel it, and reality returns. Dale Zug, my sexy boy of summer, is carrying concealed, and all my romantic fantasies, all my schoolgirl notions about a bright future together are blown right out of the water.

MY PEOPLE

A friend and I were shopping the other day at one of those eclectic gift stores that sell everything from exotic Roman glass jewelry and fart-putty to hand-crafted gutting knives alongside the latest Webkins.

"Oh look, they have mezuzahs," my friend said, pointing to a row of small, intricately carved cases displayed on a wall.

"What's a mezuzah?" I asked.

"You know what a mezuzah is," she said, "Your people invented them."

My people?

Later, I learned that "mezuzah," which means "doorpost" in Hebrew, is a piece of parchment, usually kept in a small decorative case, and inscribed with verses from a Jewish prayer. Jews affix it to the doorframe of their homes to fulfill a Biblical commandment. But what did this have to do with me?

It turns out that my friend was referring to the time I told her that I was half Jewish on my dad's side, though when I said I was half Jewish, what I really meant was that I liked gefilte fish. Growing up, my family didn't have any religion, just twice as many holidays and warring sects of recipes—Christmas, strawberry-banana salad; Hanukah, kugel; Easter, ham; Passover, Manischewitz . . . When I was seven, my family moved across the country and away from my Jewish grandparents, so after that we were down to just Christmas and Easter, but those were about presents and chocolate, not religion.

But my friend got me thinking. If Jews weren't my people,

then who were? What ethnic or cultural group did I identify with? The obvious choices didn't resonate. I'm white, for example, but I never really thought of myself as white so much as pasty, with the kind of lifeless complexion associated with corpses. My people were corpses? I don't think so.

I'm also American, but unless you leave the country, that's hardly a distinction. I have been to Canada a few times, and once to Tijuana where I threw up in a hot tub, which strikes me as a particularly American thing to do, but still, I don't really think of myself in terms of my nationality. I could just lump myself in with other middle-aged woman, which would mean that a lot of my people are experiencing the change of life, with its accompanying hot flashes, soul searching, and roller coaster of emotions. Frankly, though, between my own crying jags and inability to confront my mortality, I just can't deal with a bunch of moody women right now, let alone claim them as my own. After I learned what a mezuzah was, and that Jews had them and I didn't, I felt jealous and a bit left out. It bothered me, this realization that I couldn't readily identify my people.

So I decided to look around for them. No matter, I told myself, that I didn't feel an affinity with those big, obvious cultural or demographic groups. I would find other people, people with behaviors and characteristics that evoked in me a true sense of familiarity and kinship.

Shortly thereafter, I was in line at the corner drugstore, waiting to replace my prescription anti-aging face cream. My three cups of morning coffee were wearing off, and the woman in front of me was taking forever, jabbering on to the pharmacist and the teenage cashier about her eighty-four-year-old mother's high blood pressure and water pills, all the while blocking the register and holding up the line.

"If she takes her pill in the morning, then she don't get the dizziness," the woman volunteered, "but if she forgets, or won't do what the nurses tell her, then her ankles blow up and get all hard and shiny like them rubber doughnuts . . ." The pharmacist listened patiently, offering a sympathetic comment now and then, while the hapless cashier avoided my glare. Adolescence had not been kind to the girl, I noted, a fact that she tried to disguise by wearing theatrical make- up, dying her long hair jet black, and inserting a metal stud just beneath her lower lip.

The woman in front of me continued on about her mother, "so then we started giving her a pill in a tablespoon of apple butter, but that made her stools turn real soft, and you know those visiting nurses charge extra if she has the diarrhea."

Ugh. I made a display of checking my watch and sighing as loudly as I could. This is exactly why the giant drugstore chains are putting the little corner drugstores out of business, I fumed. The chains know how to design a real pharmacy, with separate pick-up windows and mazes behind the counter to discourage all contact between the pharmacists and the public.

About six centuries later, the woman in front of me zipped her checkbook and other belongings into her fanny pack and left, happy as you please. Meanwhile, thanks to her and her crotchety eighty-four-year-old mother, I'd never be able to eat apple butter again.

At the counter, I must have looked as annoyed as I felt. "Sorry for the wait," the teenage cashier said quietly. She took my prescription and scurried it over to the pharmacist, clearly eager to get away from me. Something about her anxious manner stirred a flash of foresight. In just a few short years, I realized, this could be my own reserved young daughter, except for the chin stud, of course, which would only happen over my dead body. But that's when it hit me.

I was the type of person who intimidated cashiers. I was one of those people you see in store lines everywhere, acting all put upon when the old person ahead of them pulls out a clawful of coupons, or when the mom with her kindergartner lets the kid pay with nickels from his own allowance. My God, it occurred to me, my own elderly mother needed water pills, yet this was my behavior. So did this mean that these—these heavy-sighing watch-checkers—were my people?

The weeks following my trip to the pharmacy were filled with equally disturbing insights into the type of person I really was.

I caught myself lying to a fundraiser who was phoning on behalf of the Volunteer Firefighter's Association, telling him that I wasn't me and didn't know when I'd be back.

Money's tight right now, I rationalized, which was true, but then I remembered my prescription anti-aging face cream, which costs ninety dollars a tube, and how careless I am with candles.

I did a load of laundry and knowingly used my favorite "ocean breeze" detergent, even though my husband has claimed repeatedly that it irritates his skin. Who gets irritated by ocean breezes? I thought defensively. But what if I was wrong? What if I really was giving my husband a skin rash?

I grew even more concerned as my list of bad behaviors just kept accruing. When a recently divorced friend poured her heart out to me over the phone, I secretly caught up on emails. I drank milk out of the jug and then put it back in the fridge. And in my heart of hearts, I knew that I really didn't want Michael Phelps to win that eighth gold medal in the Olympics. Why should he get all the glory? I thought with resentment. Why can't a bunch of corporate sponsors pay me millions of dollars to swim on TV, which would take a lot more courage than Michael Phelps, given how I look in a bathing suit?

I did, thank goodness, recognize at least one redeeming behavior on my part. In the grocery store parking lot, I returned my shopping cart to the drop-off area, something I never fail to do, even when I'm running late, even when my daughters were babies and stuck in their car seats in the broiling heat. This had to count for something, I thought, but not much, I knew, because I only did it out of paranoia that I was being secretly taped by one of those cable TV news exposés — *Tonight on Fox 29: People with bad behavior and no excuses!*

With a mixture of sadness and alarm, I confronted the ugly truth. So these were my people: a bunch of liars and sneaks who only act decently in order to placate their personality disorders. No wonder I'd never given them much thought before, I realized. I couldn't stand a single one of them.

But then I fixed myself a lox and bagel sandwich and cheered up. Because who was to say that I couldn't change? Who was to say that I couldn't disassociate myself from all those obnoxious types in my past, and become a better, more patient, less jealous-type person?

At the kitchen table, I took a bite of my sandwich and raised my jug of milk in a gesture of resolve. Here's to the future, I toasted, imagining all the ways that I would change my behavior starting today, or maybe tomorrow. Here's to my new people, I thought with a fresh sense hope; people just like me, only different; people just like me, only better.

ALMOST A CLEAN GETAWAY

The news was disturbing, but not entirely unexpected: my mother had fallen into her kitchen sink. As she explained it to me over the phone long distance, she was standing on the sink's lip, precariously stretched upwards to wipe the dust from the blinds over the window, when . . . well, when the inevitable happened. My mother was, after all, seventy-four at the time, and lacked depth perception in one eye.

So down she went, somehow ending up with her left knee wedged against the faucet, her bottle of Windex bouncing off the kitchen counter and skittering across the freshly scrubbed linoleum.

My oldest sister—the only one of my four siblings with the maturity to speak the truth to my mother—went over to my mom's house and told her she needed to hire a housecleaner.

"Bullshit," my mother answered. She gripped the handle of her favorite Swiffer, using it as a cane-slash-wetmop. "I can clean my own damn house."

Truer words were never spoken. My mother has always kept an immaculate home. When I was growing up, she Lysoled and Windexed and scrubbed everything—floors, pots and pans, pets. Every morning before going to her job as a first-grade teacher, she vacuumed and dusted and straightened the rooms, refusing to come home to a mess.

And like most clean-freaks and first-grade teachers, my mother expected others, meaning her poor, defenseless children, to abide by her housekeeping rules, as well as finish her sentences. *"Shoes off . . ."* she'd draw out the last word, similar to how the players gave clues on Password.

"*. . . in the house,*" I would finish for her, resentfully slipping off my grassy Keds by the front door for the minute or less it took to pee in the powder room, rinse my hands, and make sure there wasn't any lingering muddy suds on the Ivory soap. Filth was my mom's nemesis, and I'm not talking porn.

About six weeks after my mother fell into the sink, my husband drove me and our two daughters (ages seven and nine, at the time) to Pennsylvania to visit my mom for the long Easter weekend. Since my father's stroke a few years earlier, she had lived alone in the same house where I grew up; or rather, she lived with her beloved dogs, Hannah, a small, reddish mutt with a sweet disposition, and Sir Isaac, an insane black Lab. As far back as I can remember, my mother has always owned black dogs *and* spotless white carpets, her adaptation of the feminist credo—Yes, you can have it all, as long as you're a maniacal housekeeper.

Almost as soon as we arrived at her house, my mother, still limping from her fall, insisted on pulling up the leg of her jeans to show me her injury, even though I assured her this wasn't necessary. The entire lower half of her left leg was swollen and dark purple, like an obscenely overgrown eggplant.

"Gross," I said, but nothing more. Advising my mother to see a doctor—similar to the suggestion that she hire a cleaning woman—would not be prudent. My mother was a modern woman. She watched *Judge Judy* on the latest iteration of flat-screen TV. She used more profanity than a rap star. She was among the first in her town to be spray-tanned. Nevertheless, she hated doctors, and was convinced that they made things worse.

Despite the unsettling image of my mother's injured leg, it was nice to be back in my childhood home.

The April weather was warm, the crocuses and daffodils in full bloom. My mother had jam-packed the refrigerator with my family's favorite foods. Beside my bed, she had stacked a selection of new, hardcover books from Costco, the kind of page-turners we both liked to read, though lately her eyesight demanded large print.

As usual, my mother insisted on buying me things. "But I don't need to go shopping," I made a show of resisting.

"Bullcrap," she responded. "You need new clothes. And get those little girls some presents from me."

On the Sunday of our visit, the Easter Bunny came! Apparently, Steve and my mother, both early risers, had actually caught a glimpse of him hopping away. The girls ran around the house hunting for Easter eggs while Sir Isaac, contained in his travel cage in the basement, whined and barked in frustration.

"Isaac, Shut up!" my mother yelled. "I'm going to kill that dog."

"Remember, we don't say shut up in our house," I whispered to my seven-year-old daughter. By now, we were standing in the kitchen, inspecting her Easter basket loaded with shiny, foil-wrapped chocolates, speckled robin's eggs, and jellybeans.

My mother smiled as she peeled hard-boiled eggs for her "famous" potato salad. "I bet the Easter Bunny left you one more surprise," she said to my daughter. As if on cue, my older girl came into the kitchen carrying a big box with her name marked on it in purple crayon. Inside was a hollow milk chocolate rabbit displayed behind the cellophane window.

"Help me look for my box!" my younger daughter invited. Her excitement brought back memories of my own childhood Easters. If we happened to find a sibling's big chocolate rabbit, the rule was that we weren't allowed to move it from its hiding spot, but of course my middle sister, who grew up to be an assistant district attorney and wire tapping specialist in the nation's number one murder capital, usually found mine first and stole it.

My daughter and I searched for her rabbit in the bathtub, the laundry basket, inside the kitchen cupboards. From there, we moved on to more discreet hiding places, but something was amiss.

Under my mom's bed, I found, not a chocolate bunny, but a dust bunny, all too familiar in my own house, but here in my mother's spotless home? I also noticed something sticky—an overlooked spill?—that had hardened next to her bed. Downstairs, in the "formal" living room, the furniture showed a film of dust, and the carpeting—on closer inspection—looked more gray than white, the stair treads worn, with traces of black and reddish fur gathered around the base of the banisters.

"Here it is!" my daughter called excitedly from the dining room. She had found a box with her name on it hidden behind a large ficus tree in a corner of the room. My mother had had this tree for decades, but I noticed now that the plant's usually green leaves showed curled, yellowed tips. From lack of watering? I wondered.

Monday morning, it was time for my family to head back to Vermont. Steve loaded the car with our Easter goodies and new purchases and a giant cooler of leftover food. The kids ran around the front yard, while my mom insisted on writing Steve and me a check—if she could ever find her damn checkbook. Already, my mom had filled a bucket of suds and left it on the kitchen floor, in anticipation of cleaning after our departure.

In the front yard, Sir Isaac raced around, even more hyper than usual. The night before, he had eaten an entire bag of jellybeans left on the kitchen counter. Steve and the girls hugged my mom goodbye, while I tried not to show that I was crying. Ever since I moved away from my childhood home over two decades ago, I have cried when saying goodbye to my parents. Yet this time it felt like a deeper, real sadness, rather than just sentimental habit.

My mom and I exchanged a quick hug — we both felt awkward at goodbyes — and I caught a whiff of Lysol on the cuff of her sweatshirt. I got in the car and Steve started to pull out of the driveway, but not before my mom dropped a check for five hundred dollars through my open window and onto my lap. She had filled in the numeric amount and signed it in her shaky script, but left it to me to write in the rest.

"Don't argue with me," she cut off my lame protest, limping toward the house as fast as she could. I watched her go, followed by her crazy black dog, and told myself that everything, almost, was as it should be.

Strangers on a Train

Normally, I sleep peacefully through much of the eight-hour train ride from my home in Vermont to my mom's house in Pennsylvania. I wake from one nap and the scenery is open farmland. Minutes, or maybe hours later, I doze off again to a backdrop of graffiti-scarred warehouses. It's as if I'm unconsciously absorbing America's Northeast Corridor in all its splendor and squalor, similar to how I used to go to bed with a dictionary under my pillow in the hopes of improving my vocabulary.

But the last time I took this eight-hour train ride my sleep was fitful at best. The day before my trip, I experienced the worst hangover of my life, either that or a case of food poisoning. I had gone to a Midsummer's Night dance party under the stars. The food and drink table was poorly illuminated, just a row of Tiki torches to help me stumble my way to the multitude of open bottles of wine.

Around two in the morning as the party was winding down (or maybe I was the last to leave), I stuffed down a hoagie from the picked-over sandwich tray. My reasoning was that this would offset any effects of the alcohol. Not that I was drunk, I told myself, as I sang my way to where I thought I had left my car.

On the train thirty-six hours later, my right eyeball still throbbed and my stomach continued to spasm, although by now it felt as hollow as a dried gourd. For the first time ever, I was painfully aware of the train's confined quarters. The air smelled stale, like a close talker with a medical condition was exhaling in my face. A man seated nearby slept with his mouth open; his face bore the dull sheen of gummy bears. The woman next to him scratched her forearm, and I could see the spray of dead skin cells circulating my way. It was as if I had developed super-sensory powers, only these were the kind of super powers you would be given in hell.

I tried gazing out the window, but instead of the usual soporific effect, the flashing scene-scapes only made my head hurt worse. A phlegmy cough erupted from somewhere behind me. Across the aisle, a woman bulging from her tube top faced me in one of those backwards seats. She tore open a Snickers bar and took a bite. Too late, I averted my eyes. With my new super powers, I could see in my mind's eye the chocolate nougat (packed with peanuts!) filling the indents of her molars, then mixing with the half-digested contents of her stomach, still identifiable — ugh! — as the Meat Lovers Platter at Denny's.

All my life I have suffered from a too-vivid imagination. To offset the mental havoc this can cause, I often try to soothe myself through deep breathing. Inhale through the nose. Exhale through the mouth. Today, unfortunately, this tactic was of no use, given that I was trying not to breathe at all. I needed another relaxation technique, something to empty my head of disturbing images and calm my overactive gag reflex.

Halle Berry!

Halle Berry's face popped into my mind, maybe because she had recently graced the cover of *People* magazine. Looks-wise, I have always thought she is the most perfect person on the planet. Toffee-colored skin. Silky hair. A dazzling smile with any hint of saliva airbrushed away.

Halle Berry . . . Halle Berry . . . Halle Berry . . . I fixed her image in my mind and eventually managed to doze.

As the train approached Hartford, Connecticut, the conductor requested that all passengers sitting alone remove their belongings from the seat beside them. We needed to make room for the new arrivals. Groggy, but feeling more myself, I grabbed my purse and laptop bag from the overhead rack and deposited them on the empty seat next to me.

Out of the corner of my eye, I watched the travelers file past, a parade of inner thighs rubbing beneath too short shorts, pot bellies hanging over belts, a grungy teenager in a tank top and sweatpants. Just the word—*sweat*pants! I tried not to be judgmental, after all, my own thighs rub, but the world was still too much with me.

A Muslim woman wearing a heavy black veil and robes paused beside my seat. I stared down at my sneakers, hoping she wouldn't sit next to me. It's not that I have a problem with Muslims or their faith, which likely holds more logic than my own belief in some omniscient power that remains benevolent, as long as I knock on wood or don't get too full of myself.

What I can't fathom, however, is the way certain religious types dress. I grew up in Lancaster, Pennsylvania, Amish country, where it was hard enough during the hot, humid summers to look at the women in their black, aproned dresses and stockings and not feel vicarious heat prostration. But Muslim women! Covered from head to toe in so much cloth, Muslim women make the Amish look like streetwalkers.

Thanks to my new guardian angel, Halle Berry, or maybe the fact that I was still experiencing tremors in my hands, this particular Muslim woman thought better than to ask me to move my belongings, and took a seat a few rows ahead of me in the train car.

By the time we reached New Haven, I couldn't wait any longer. I needed to go pee. My lingering dizziness and the sway of the car forced me to grip the seatbacks on my way to the bathroom. En route, it occurred to me that, for all my lack of knowledge of the human anatomy, the one thing I wished I did *not* remember was that skin is the biggest organ. I could just feel the germs—viruses, flesh-eating bacteria, e-coli—permeating my palms. Worse yet, in the bathroom I was forced to grip the handrail as I squatted above the toilet, either that or risk direct contact with the backs of my thighs. Call it exhaustion or post-traumatic stress disorder, but when I returned to my seat I managed to pass out for a time, until the screech of brakes woke me when the train pulled into New York City's Penn Station.

"Is this seat taken?" A forty-something man wearing a summer business suit and trendy eyeglasses directed the question either to me or the person on his Bluetooth. New Yorkers, of course, can see through clever ploys like faking a seatmate, so I had no choice but to move my belongings and allow him to sit beside me. Thank goodness he was a metrosexual, one of those impeccably groomed males who are not afraid of nose hair clippers or pore-reducing skin toner.

At first, the man ignored me, the way only New Yorkers can ignore people who don't matter. But then he stood up to retrieve something from the overhead rack and there, eye level, not two feet from my face, was the front panel of his tan, linen trousers—his zipper at half-mast.

Sexual pheromones aside, when it comes right down to it, certain male body parts are not attractive, at least not when you are recovering from a hangover-slash-food-poisoning. With my new super-sensory powers, I could see right through the lightweight fabric of his dress pants and designer briefs. The man sat down just a few seconds later, obscuring his lap with his *New York Times*, but the image of his private parts nestled in a pallet of pubic hair had already imprinted itself in my mind.

Halle Berry! Halle Berry! Halle Berry!

This time, her image failed to comfort. My stomach gur-
gled, bringing back all-too-vivid memories of yesterday,
and how much of it had been spent dry heaving over our ill-
conceived low-flush toilet. Today, however, I had managed to
drink plenty of juice and eat a personal pan pizza from the café
car, all without incident. But had I been too optimistic? Just
the idea of being sick and stuck in a window seat convinced
me that I needed to throw up. Under normal circumstances, I
would have bolted for the bathroom, but this meant squeezing
past my seatmate and his metrosexual package.

By now, my super powers had kicked into overdrive. Every
sensation, every image, every aspect of the human condition
felt magnified. I needed to empty my mind, to create a mental
space devoid of sensory stimulation and the vagaries of my
own imagination. A few rows in front of me, the Muslim
woman stood out among all the other bare-headed passengers.
I rested my gaze on the back of her black veil and, for once,
saw her head covering not as sign of suppression, but as a
relief from having to look at everybody else's exposed hair.

By the time the train reached Philadelphia, my metrosexual
seatmate was nowhere to be seen. Apparently, he had slipped
away quietly after I had drifted back to sleep. Now it was time
for me to leave the train, too, to complete the last leg of my
trip to Lancaster. I stood up, feeling considerably steadier on
my feet. My right eye no longer throbbed and my stomach felt
settled. What's more, everybody, everything, had returned to
normal proportions. My super powers from hell were gone.

I retrieved my belongings from the overhead rack and
started walking down the aisle toward the exit. Next to the
Muslim woman's seat, I hesitated. Normally, I would have
passed right by her, this stranger on a train whose life seemed
so remote from my own. Instead, I felt a sudden urge to

connect, to thank her for being there in my time of need, or at least ask her how she was holding up in the heat. But of course that would have been too weird. I was a Western woman with modern proclivities. I drank alcohol and cavorted under the stars. A sheik could offer me ten million dollars and I still would not cover my head and body in the name of religion. Still, before I left the train, I tried to catch the woman's lowered eyes, hoping to exchange a smile.

CRIMINAL MINDS

In the center of my Vermont village — on the same stretch of Main Street where you'll find the library built in 1893, the congregational church, the historical society, the locally owned mini-mart, the Elks Lodge, and the Praise Chapel with a sign offering inspirational outreach every time you drive by (*Feeling down? Look up!*) — once stood a popular diner that made someone in our town mad enough to commit arson!

The story begins circa World War II, when the diner was built on the corner of the village's only busy intersection. Perched on a narrow patch of land set close to the road, the glass-and-panel doors of the diner faced Main Street, while its backside bordered a steep slope overlooking the White River.

Thanks to its rib-sticking fare, bottomless cups of coffee, and friendly atmosphere, the diner proved a popular establishment for locals and flatlanders alike. Then decades passed, the vinyl booths cracked, the mugs chipped, and the big, black clock with a face yellowed from decades of cigarette smoke, saw fewer and fewer customers.

After the diner closed, the building fell into disrepair, until several years later when a fellow from the neighboring town bought the shabby eatery on the overgrown lot. The newspaper reported that he had plans to renovate and reopen it as soon as possible. This was good news indeed for a Main Street feeling its age. Once a center of business and industry in the nineteenth century, the village had lost much of its bustle after several nearby mills and industries shut down. While fixing up the small establishment might not revitalize the village to its glory days, it offered at least the equivalent of a hip replacement.

Almost from the get-go the diner's new owner and town officials didn't see eye to eye. They wrangled over zoning permits and safety codes. The reconstruction—part of which involved stabilizing the slope behind the diner so that it wouldn't collapse into the river—ground to an angry halt. While previously the abandoned diner had simply looked forlorn and unkempt, this gutted iteration projected an angry, defiant edge. The owner left the site a wasteland of haphazardly piled concrete slabs and abandoned earth movers, and covered the exposed plywood with green plastic garbage bags.

By now, the stand-off between the town and the diner's owner had been going on for over four years, with both parties resorting to lots of legal motions and strong language. Town members gathered signatures on a petition at the library, demanding something be done about this festering problem. Finally, after so much time and so little progress, someone took matters into his or her own hands.

But who? Who set fire to the old diner? Suspects were plentiful, though the authorities never made an arrest.

Maybe it was the librarian who solicited all those signatures on the petition, or the mini-mart manager, confronted with a view of the ruined structure every time he looked out his window. Maybe it was the minister of the congregational church believing he was doing God's work, or the husband and wife pastors at the Praise Chapel, extending their outreach in new directions. It could have been one of the old timers at the Elks Lodge; no one could accuse them of being pushovers. Even as their lodge faced extinction because of diminished membership, they refused to yield when some wives made a bid to join the fraternity. This couldn't have made things pleasant at home.

Maybe the fire was set by a member of the town selectboard, emboldened by the power of the office. Or maybe the curator at the historical society saw fit to make history rather than simply archive it. It might even have been set by a firefighter. It was reported that the structure burned front to back and left to right, producing a big, black cloud of smoke that rose high in the October air, a strong indication that the blaze was petroleum-fueled. According to the fire marshal, it was just lucky such fast-moving flames, punctuated by two booming explosions, failed to leap across the street to the self-serve gas pumps at the mini mart. But was it luck . . . or the design of an arsonist who knew how to set a contained fire?

Every one of the several hundred citizens, neighbors, and friends who signed the petition had a motive. I signed the petition myself. It could have been me who struck the match. One thing was certain: it had to be somebody.

By the time I drove my daughters, ages eight and six at the time, home from school the afternoon of the fire, the structure was nothing but a pile of rubble and smoldering ash. The girls rubbernecked as I slowed the car to a crawl, though there wasn't much left to see.

"Mommy," the six-year-old asked, "Did you burn the Monstrosity down?" This was the name I had dubbed the building, not because it was physically imposing, but because its ugliness loomed large in my mind.

I admitted I had no alibi. I also made no secret about how much I hated the Monstrosity. A month or so before the diner burned, my daughter asked me to stop ranting about it every time we passed the structure on our way to school.

"But it's just awful having that thing in the center of the village," I had responded. "It's a travesty. Someone should do something about this!"

"You've already said that a million times," my daughter said.

"I ought to burn the Monstrosity down!" I announced. "I'd be doing everybody a favor."

"Just stop, Mommy. Please, stop."

That's when I realized I wasn't just annoying my children, I was frightening them. I might even be causing them psychological harm. *Was Mommy going to do something bad?* From that point forward, I decided to keep my thoughts about the Monstrosity to myself.

Whenever a crime is committed in small-town America, people always seem to react with surprise, as if criminal minds can't foment in places with well water. This mentality is no different in my neck of the woods. I was reminded of this when I read a quote in the newspaper from a farmer who lives in Tunbridge, a town about twenty or so miles up the White River from mine, population 3,900. "When you're living in the middle of Tunbridge," the farmer remarked, "you shouldn't have to worry about someone driving by and shooting your cow with a 9mm gun."

No, you shouldn't, I agreed, but then again, where should you have to worry about such a thing?

I remember the first time I committed a crime, ironically in a small Vermont village not unlike the one where I live today. I was a high school senior in Pennsylvania on a school trip to learn how to ski. In the resort's gift shop, I stole two expensive winter hats, one for me and one for my boyfriend back home. My shoplifting days are long gone, but I still harbor my share of criminal impulses. Who doesn't find themselves entertaining dark, lawless thoughts, regardless of where they call home?

After the diner was destroyed, the Monstrosity's owner accused the fire chief of letting the building burn, rather than trying to save it. "You don't let the fire burn the building down, and then spray water on it," the owner was quoted in the newspaper. In the same article, he said that he was going to try to get town officials to pay for a new building, but if they weren't willing to "sit down and rationalize this with them," he was going to sue.

In fact, he did more than that. Served with papers demanding he clean up the site and start working on his proposed diner by a certain deadline, the owner began construction anew. Within days, he had hammered together a lopsided box of a building, adding a jutting front that served no purpose but one. Now, thanks to this new feature, the Monstrosity severely obstructed the view of drivers wanting to turn left onto Main Street. This time, the owner weatherized the building's exterior by tacking on some cheap plastic sheeting. On windy days, the plastic billowed out like sails, reducing visibility from poor to next to impossible.

Six years have passed since someone burned down the original diner, laying the foundation for the owner to build the existing Monstrosity. Every so often he adds new touches to the structure and site, usually after town officials chide him for his lack of progress. For a while he stockpiled more concrete slabs taken from disassembled bridges. Later, he sheathed some poles near the roof with empty beer cans. At one point, passersby were treated to the sight of a toilet plunked in the middle of the muddy lot. I can just imagine how that toilet goaded the arsonist.

My children still suspect I had a hand in the fire. What can I say, other than the fact that they needn't check my purse for accelerant. As Einstein once said, the definition of insanity is doing the same thing over and over again while expecting different results. I can assure them my sanity is intact.

Why burn the place to the ground again, when the owner would only replace it with something worse?

Still, something has to be done.

Yesterday, the same as every day, I needed to turn left at the intersection onto Main Street. As I inched my way forward into oncoming traffic, straining to see around the wall of the Monstrosity, a car whizzed by nearly striking my bumper. This, of course, was nothing new. Everyone in town knows this corner is an accident waiting to happen.

In fact, it occurred to me, an accident at this intersection wouldn't necessarily be a bad thing. Unlike the fire, with its unforeseen consequences, a tragic accident would leave the Monstrosity's owner no room for recourse. The public outcry would be so great the structure would have to be destroyed. And in its place, I envisioned, the town could establish a small park, one with a lovely stone bench in memoriam to the accident victim. Where the toilet once stood, the ladies of the town garden club could plant pretty flowers.

But who should be the victim of this tragic accident? It wouldn't do to sacrifice my own life, given that I was the mother of two children who needed me. Nor did I want to cut short anyone else's bright future. But what if the accident involved just the right person?

Like so many small towns, ours is populated with a disproportionate number of elderly folk. The young people tend to escape to the glamour of the big cities, leaving civic-minded seniors to continue running the church suppers and clothing drives. All it would take is one committed volunteer, say a centenarian diagnosed with just weeks, maybe days, to live. The end would be quick, the service to our community great. Neighbors helping neighbors, everybody doing their part for the greater good, isn't that what small-town America is all about?

Of course, if such a volunteer wasn't forthcoming, someone—maybe the town librarian, or the mini-mart manager, or a member of the Elks—could take matters into his or her own hands.

"You're invited to a special event in the village!" this someone could call up the oldest person he or she knew, preferably one who should have given up his license years ago. "Your friends and neighbors would like you to talk about the good old days." Hearing this, the old person's spirits would lift, at this reminder that he had not outlived his usefulness.

"The location of this special event is easy to find," the caller, who really could be anyone—the minister at the congregational church, a select board member, me—would continue. "Just head to the old diner at the center of town. You remember the old diner with its big, black clock with the yellowed face, and its bottomless cup of coffee?"

At this point in the conversation the caller might pause, taking a moment to imagine the scene—the jutting wall of the Monstrosity, the billowing plastic, the almost blind driver approaching the blind intersection . . . And, after that, a park bench and flowers.

"Just turn left onto Main Street," the caller would encourage, "and once you try to do that, we're almost home free."

A FEW MINUTES OF MY TIME

I am not the self-service type, having spent years perfecting the art of learned helplessness. At the airport, for example, I shun the self check-in option and prefer to wait in line for a human baggage checker, keeping company with all the other technosaurs and curmudgeons muttering things like, "Walter, go see what the hold up is, we've only got four hours until our flight."

Given that I can't or won't handle even the most basic technical tasks, the first thing I did when my laptop died was to phone my computer guy.

"It turns on, but nothing shows up on the screen," I tell him.

"What kind of computer is it?" my computer guy asks. "A laptop," I reply impatiently. Even I know that much.

My computer guy is really nice, but sometimes I get the feeling he's trying to avoid me. After walking me through the steps to determine the brand (something called a "Hewlett-Packard"), he insists I'd be better off calling the company's technical support center. Then he hangs up.

He has got to be kidding! I'd rather phone my mother-in-law and listen to her retell the story of how she saved $1.25 on a box of fire logs by going to four different malls. With no alternative, I dial Hewlett-Packard's 1-800 number. "Due to heavy call volume, all of our lines are busy," a recording tells me. Now what does that say about the company's quality control? I fume. My laptop shouldn't even be on the fritz, given that it's only three years old, and my mother paid good money to buy it for me.

Finally, someone takes my call. "I apologize for the delay," says an accented voice. "My name is Prakash. How may I help?"

Oh good lord. I have enough trouble understanding foreigners face to face, let alone across phone lines. I tell him about my blank screen.

Prakash requests that I unplug my computer's power cord and remove the battery.

"Battery? What battery?" If I had wanted to know about the inner workings of my laptop, I would have looked at the manual. Then I would have killed myself.

Prakash informs me that he will need to run a remote diagnostic test. "This will require a few more minutes of your time," he apologizes. While he runs the test we wait in silence, until it feels too weird, like two heavy breathers on the same line.

"Where exactly are you located?" I ask, having read that most American computer companies try to save big bucks by basing their call centers overseas.

"India," he says.

Oh. I can't help but think of the recent terrorist attacks there. "I'm sorry for your country's tragedy." I don't refer to Mumbai specifically because I'm afraid I'll mispronounce the word.

"You know of the attacks?" he sounds surprised. "Do you subscribe to the Indian news channels?"

At first I don't understand his question. Then I catch on. "No, the attacks were all over the American news." Could people in other countries really think that Americans are that self-absorbed as to ignore world events of this magnitude?

Prakash shares that he is from Mumbai.

"I hope you and your family were safe," I say. Suddenly, what was just another horrendous headline has a real person attached to it, or at least a real voice at a technical support center.

"We were fortunate," Prakash responds. Then he tells me that my computer has failed the diagnostic test. It will require a new hard drive.

"How much will that cost me?" I try to keep my irritation in check. What if my city had been attacked by terrorists? I think. What if gunmen had seized the White River train station or the Hotel Coolidge ten minutes from my house? The last thing I would need is some woman from thousands of miles away giving me grief about her laptop.

"I will be happy to find that information for you," Prakash says. "May I have just a few more minutes of your time?"

It turns out that a replacement hard drive will cost about $300. When I ask Prakash for advice, he suggests I consider purchasing a new computer. Hewlett-Packard is having a sale, so I could get a better laptop with free upgrades at a very good price. "Shall I connect you to our Home Office Store?" he asks.

By now, the last thing I want to do is spend more time on the phone talking about stupid computers. I have things to do. Without a working laptop, I have an excuse to take the afternoon off, watch a movie, or maybe take a long nap. Still, I find myself saying yes. Before Prakash transfers me to a sales agent, I tell him to take care. I want to say more, do something to convince him that I really am sorry for his country's tragedy, but what?

When I hang up the phone a few minutes later, I am the owner of a brand new HP Pavilion dv5z Entertainment Notebook with a Windows 32-bit Vista® Home Premium operating system, 3GB DDR2 System Memory, and Wireless-G Card. I have no idea what any of this means. I also can't really afford a new computer, and suspect that my regular computer guy could have fixed my old laptop for considerably less. Still, I feel better having spent the $649 plus tax, a small price to pay to offset my feelings of learned helplessness.

A Real American Idol

A few summers ago, my two daughters and I went to the *American Idol* concert at the DCU Center in Worcester, Massachusetts, over two hours from where we live. This was the closest venue that wasn't sold out by the time I called for tickets, so I bought three seats for an exorbitant price. I love American Idol, mostly because the show takes nobodies and turns them into instant mega-stars, which is something I constantly fantasize for myself.

The DCU Center — billed the nation's premier entertainment complex — accommodates 11,000 attendees. As it turned out, 10,998 of them had better seats than us. My daughters and I were stuck in the highest row, so close to the roof rafters we could hit our heads on them. Plus, we were so far to the rear of the stage that we couldn't even watch the concert on the giant projection screen suspended from the ceiling, given that we were seated behind it.

While we waited for the concert to begin, the girls spotted two empty seats one tier below, so they moved down, figuring they could always leave if the real ticket holders showed up. I probably could have found a better seat as well, but stayed put, preferring to be a martyr than a squatter (though I did refuse to give up the binoculars).

Right after my daughters abandoned me, who should appear but the man and woman with the only two seats worse than mine. They carried cardboard trays loaded with food and sodas, and had bought one of those commemorative American Idol books with glossy pictures of the performers and their bios.

The woman sat beside me, securing her Big Chug between her thick thighs. "Is this your first time?" she asked me.

"First time?" I asked.

"We saw the concert in Manchester a couple weeks ago," she enthused. "It's a great show!"

What are you so happy about? I wanted to ask. You have the absolute worst seats in the house, the last thing you need is that Big Chug, and nobody except maybe Erin Brockovich is going to care whether you get cancer from inhaling all these loose paint flakes on the rafters. Still, I kept my thoughts to myself, rather than risk appearing judgmental.

The woman and her companion started chowing down on their nachos and hot dogs, while skimming through her commemorative book. I tried to snatch glances of them, too, but her super-sized breasts didn't make it any easier.

Eventually, the house lights dimmed and one of the performers — the first of the ten finalists to get voted out of the competition — came onto the stage. Clearly, I had time to kill, given that I'd only come to see the winner. I'd voted for him every week during the show because he was a good singer, and because he'd suffered the most tragedy in his life.

I scoped out the audience with my binoculars. This was a G-rated crowd, full of parents and kids (sitting in their own seats, I presumed). One tier below me, people in wheelchairs had their own section, with a terrific view of the stage. Maybe I'd get lucky next concert, I mused, and be hit by a bus and paralyzed from the waist down.

Near center stage, a sea of young people in identical blue t-shirts hogged a primo section of seats. Probably some church youth group, I assessed. So why weren't they out working for Habitat for Humanity or some other do-gooder cause? Considering the cost of all those American Idol tickets, they could have built an entire bedroom community in El Salvador.

And there! In the very first row! A baby on its mother's lap! And it wasn't even listening to the concert, thanks to a pair of noise-canceling headphones protecting its delicate baby ears.

The singers came and went, but I couldn't stop obsessing about the audience. Why should all these people have better seats than me? I fumed. It's not like they were celebrities or VIPs. These were just ordinary folks, the kind of people I needed to feel superior to, otherwise I felt ordinary myself.

Normally, I have no trouble honing in on other people's inferior qualities. *Sure,* I tell myself, *that woman is better looking than me, but at least I don't have downy arms.* Or, *So what if that writer has more talent; who wants the hassle of a second home in the Keys?* But tonight, I felt like the loser among 11,000 people, including Mr. and Mrs. Big Chug whooping it up beside me.

Eventually, the winner of American Idol came onto the stage and everybody cheered. A young man with Downs Syndrome raced to the railing of the nosebleed section. He wore a t-shirt with an image of the singer's face, tucked into white shorts worn way too high. When the winner started singing, the young man danced and played air guitar, just like a developmentally disabled rock star.

It must be nice, I thought sarcastically, to be so oblivious; to not care about all the things that other people have that you don't, including the correct number of chromosomes. But then it occurred to me: Yes, yes it would be nice; not to be developmentally disabled, but to be free of jealousy and resentment. I watched the young man rock out, arms flailing, hips gyrating in his high-waisted white shorts, having the time of his life. And at that moment I felt sorrier for myself than I had the whole evening—but it had nothing to do with my lousy seat.

STILL MY DAD

My dad lived in a nursing home for six years. He wound up there because of a massive stroke that left him paralyzed on his left side and did a number on his brain. In the hospital during his long and rocky recuperation, the visiting psychiatrists weren't sure how much of his mind remained intact. When they asked him to name the Vice President of the United States, or what day Christmas fell on, often he'd stare into space. But after the psychiatrists left, I'd ask him for some five- or six-letter word I needed to complete my crossword puzzle, and plenty of times he'd give me the right answer. Then my mother would yell at him, "Myles, stop being so bullheaded."

My dad was an engineer; he designed farm equipment for New Holland Machine Company in Lancaster, Pennsylvania. After he took early retirement, but before his stroke changed everything, he had about ten great years. In retirement, my dad's social life took off. Every Wednesday at six a.m. he'd meet his buddies for breakfast at Friendly's, where they'd solve the world's problems from their regular booth. My dad competed in golf tournaments. He played Around the World with his sons and grandsons at the basketball court in the park. Occasionally, my dad would win—and gloat, as was his right as a short, pudgy, Jewish great-grandfather pushing seventy.

When I visited my parents from Vermont, my dad would take my family and I on road trips to the Philadelphia Zoo, Hershey Park, the Strasburg Railroad. He let my two little girls play horsey on his back. He chauffeured my mother and me to the mall because we both refused to drive on Route 30 with all the construction. While I tried on clothes at the Gap or Victoria's Secret, my dad loitered by the cash registers. He always insisted on paying for everything. One time we were at a drug store and I tried to sneak to the checkout to buy some tampons, but my dad intercepted me at the counter. He wouldn't let the clerk take my money.

My dad had a woodshop in his basement. He built nice things: TV cabinets, wooden-handled trays, conjoined dancing teddy bears, a sleigh bed with his grown-up grandson. "Myles," my mom would call down to him from the top of the basement stairs, "Don't track up any sawdust." My dad taught his youngest grandson to fish. He baked homemade bread two or three times a week in what had to be the world's first bread machine. He drove a friend's son to all his orthodontia appointments because the boy's mother had to work. He and my mom took bus trips to Atlantic City, to Dollywood, to see the Rockettes at Radio City Music Hall. My dad went to funerals, more and more with each passing year.

Every day, my dad walked his sweet-natured dog, Hannah, a mile to the park and back. Then he would set out again to walk Sir Isaac, the lunging black lab my mother had insisted on adopting, even though my dad didn't want him. Every day my dad made at least one, sometimes two trips to the grocery store to fetch a can of stewed tomatoes or low-fat whipped cream for some new recipe my parents wanted to try, or to pick up more laundry detergent because my mom did four loads of wash a day, even after it was just the two of them at home.

Every day, my dad worked the Jumble and the crossword puzzle in the newspaper. Every day, he would fall asleep sitting up on the couch, with *Law and Order* blaring from the TV.

But then my mom, who had watched him like a hawk since his heart attack when he was in his fifties, would call out, "Myles! Are you awake?" And if he didn't answer immediately she would yell louder, "Myles, are you all right? Wake up!"

After my dad's stroke, after weeks of ICUs and respirators, and after my mom told the hospital administrators once, then again, to resuscitate if necessary, my dad's health stabilized. But he failed to show any signs that he would regain the use of his left side or much of his independence. So my mom put my dad in a nursing home. Then she bought a $35,000 wheelchair-accessible van.

The first year my dad was in the nursing home, he drove everyone nuts. "Let's go! Let's go!" he pounded the armrest of his wheelchair with his good hand. At night, he beat on the bed rail, prompting the aides to ask, "What are we going to do with Myles? He's disturbing the other patients." My mom lived in fear the nursing home people would kick him out, like the disruptive child in day care. She was the one who had first saved his life, but when he behaved this way she'd threaten to kill him and almost mean it, at least in the heat of the moment.

For a couple years, my mom tried to bring my dad back to their house almost every day, or take him out shopping, or to lunch. Sometimes these outings were nice, but just as often they would lead to the kind of fights between my parents that used to embarrass me as a kid. My dad's good leg would start bouncing on his footrest. The fist pounding would begin. He would yell about real and imaginary pain. He would obsess about having to go to the bathroom. "Myles, be still!" my mom would shout back, "You're in the middle of Home Depot for God's sake!"

On the thirty-minute drives back to the nursing home, my dad often would be seized by dusk anxiety or some other form of panic disorder. "I'm falling!" he would cry out from the back of the van, even though he was strapped in tight. "Help me! I'm falling!" he'd smack his armrest. If I was the one behind the wheel, he would say what he always said to me since I first started driving, "Not so fast! Not so fast!"

Over the years, my dad's health went more and more downhill. He used to push himself short distances in his wheelchair, but eventually stopped trying. His eyesight deteriorated to shadows and forms. He could no longer feed himself. His face displayed the doughy pallor of a nursing home resident. He stopped having so many panic attacks, or complaining obsessively about pain, but when he did, one Oxycodone—and a word from my mom—usually set him right. For some reason, my dad found comfort in holding his toothbrush.

Year after year, my mom drove to the nursing home five mornings a week to be with my dad from seven until two in the afternoon. On Tuesdays and Thursdays, she hired a caretaker to sit with him and feed him his meals. She instructed the woman to make sure his TV set was tuned to his favorite country music channel or the ball game, and to always press the call button right before she left. My mom never wanted my dad to be alone.

When I visited from Vermont, I watched my dad nap in his leather recliner in the sunny corner of his room and I knew, or at least I hoped, that he was someplace else. Maybe the chicken farm where he grew up. Maybe playing drums in the jazz band he formed at the University of Illinois, which is what he was doing when he met my mom and stole her away from the fiancé she already had.

The stroke took away most of what my dad could do, and a lot of who he was. But even as he declined, he could still make me laugh. One visit I was looking at old photos of my dad as a boy, and I mentioned a resemblance between him and my then seven-year-old daughter. "Give her my apologies," he joked, and I felt a rush of gratitude, as I always did when I saw these glimpses of the dad I knew before he got sick. To the end, my dad still loved country music. He still favored the Cubs over the Phillies. He still had a sweet tooth and enjoyed a good cup of coffee, though it was hard for him to steady the cup. He still made my mom furious, and he still loved her and remembered to tell her so.

He was still my dad.

During my last visit with him, I sat with him in his room, while he reclined in his chair, covered in a heavy, fleece blanket. Some talk show hosts chattered away on the TV.

"Mommy and I are going shopping this afternoon," I told him, by way of making conversation. "I think I'll buy a new pair of jeans." When my dad didn't answer, I started flipping through the channels. These days he rarely responded. But a few moments later, my dad's toothbrush tapped a few times on his armrest. "Mommy's got my wallet," he said, his eyes still closed, his voice weak. "You make sure she pays for everything when you go."

TWEEN A ROCK AND A HEART PLACE

For months I had been struggling to adjust to the realities of parenting a "tween," a word my then eleven-year-old daughter forbade me to speak aloud. "I hate that word!" she announced when we were shopping at J.C. Penney's. "Never, ever say that word again!" This, after I had simply suggested we head to the Tweens section to buy her some new jeans. Who knew? I thought, as we drove home in sullen silence. I had simply been reading a sign above the clothing racks for girls sized 7 through 16.

"It's hormones," my friends with their own tweenage daughters reassured me. Eleven-year-old hormones are to blame for those radical mood swings and that look on her face that spoke volumes — *Your existence horrifies me; why can't you spontaneously combust, or at least be normal like other moms?*

Sometimes, when these hormones took over my daughter's personality, I forgot that she was even human, let alone a girl in a growing-up body. Instead, I started to think of her as one of those deceptively cute wild animals, like a dingo or capuchin monkey; one of those creatures that Ranger Rick warns against in his magazine: *Remember, readers, these adorable-looking animals do not make good pets! They can be dangerous and are better left in the wild.*

One day my daughter came home from school in another one of her moods. She dropped her overstuffed, pink backpack in the middle of the floor and headed straight to the kitchen. I had made sure it was stocked with her favorite after-school

102

snacks—Thai soup, Little Debbie coffeecakes, orange juice. Times like these, Plan A was to spike her blood sugar.

"How was your day?" I asked.

"Fine." She took her soup out of the microwave and bee-lined for her room. Plan B was to give her space.

Later that afternoon, for the sake of peace in the household, I didn't call her on her lack of "thank you" when I dropped her off at field hockey practice. I also let it go when she (once again) ignored my request to pick up the mess of paper and scissors and glue that she had left in the back room after her scrap-booking project two weeks ago.

At dinner, she kept tipping her chair back—one precarious degree away from a skull fracture—until her father told her to sit properly or go to her room. Ah! Here was my chance to be the *nice* parent; to gain a tactical advantage over my husband. For some reason, the hormones that had convinced my daughter that I was Evil Incarnate hadn't sullied her father, even when he corrected her behavior or dared to speak directly to her friends. The two of them maintained a close, easy relationship that consumed me with jealousy.

"Aren't you hungry?" I asked kindly, watching as she excavated the chicken stir-fry on her plate, flicking slivers of transparent onion off her fingers like boogers.

"It's gross," she muttered, though she had always liked this meal before. Every day my daughter was discovering a world full of new and disgusting things, mostly related to food items (mayonnaise, tomato soup, shrimp) . . . and me. The other day, me eating a sandwich with mayonnaise was enough to drive her to her piano keyboard, where she pounded out her practice music to erase the images. *The horror! The horror!* I could just see the hormones, writhing like Kurtz on his deathbed.

After dinner, my husband took our younger daughter out for ice cream, probably to escape the miasma of moodiness overhanging our house. Her older sister disappeared somewhere while I hid in my room, reading a murder mystery. Then I felt guilty. Hiding wasn't a good parenting strategy. I needed to reach out to my daughter, to try and connect with her in this new stage of her life. Besides, I missed her. When those drama queen hormones weren't around, she could be non-threatening and the kindest person I knew.

"What are you making?" I found her in her bedroom, sitting cross-legged on the hardwood floor, threading little blue beads onto a string.

"Nothing," she froze mid-bead, suddenly fixated by the needle nose pliers beside her. Translation: *Go away. Leave me alone. Why do you have to continually ruin my life?*

"Can I do some beading, too?"

"No."

"Do you want to play Monopoly later on?"

"No."

"Clue?"

"No."

My husband, a psychologist, and I had discussed the best way to handle this kind of hostile behavior. In one of his pep talks to me, he shared one of the tenets of family therapy: "Try not to take your kids' bad behavior personally. They're taking their feelings out on you, but it's not about you." I took some deep breaths, determined to remain calm, a parent in control. *It's not about me. It's not about me.*

"I'm going to make a cup of tea. Would you like one?" I offered my daughter.

"No."

Still, she refused to look at me. What was her problem? Had I grown a third eye? Did she think she would turn into stone if she looked at my face? Did it ever occur to her that I had feelings, too? Or that sometimes her behavior made me want to scream and cry and give up on our relationship?

Just in time, I remembered the hormones.

"Honey, what's the matter? I don't want to fight. I just want to spend some time with you."

"Oh. My. God!" Finally, she looked, or rather glared, at me. "You always do that! *'What's the matter? What's the matter?'*" she pitched her voice high and whiny, mocking me. "When's Daddy coming home?" Tears glazed her eyes, as if I was Mommy Dearest and her father was social services.

A scene played out in my mind. I saw myself picking up my daughter's compartmentalized bead box—a rainbow of tiny beads that she had meticulously sorted—and turn it upside down. I saw hundreds and hundreds of beads skittering in all directions, falling into the uneven gaps between her bedroom floorboards, gaps that had accumulated decades of dust, dog hairs, and other old-house detritus. Unlike mayonnaise, or even me eating mayonnaise, those gaps truly were disgusting. Yet here she sat, amid the filth and squalor, perfectly content until I came along.

"You are such a spoiled brat!" I left, slamming her bedroom door so hard it bounced back open. We have rules in our house: no slamming doors, no name-calling. I shut it hard again. My pulse was racing; maybe I was having a heart attack. If not, I would fake one, right in the hallway outside her door. That would teach her a lesson, I thought. That would serve her right. *See what you've done?* My cold, lifeless eyes would haunt her. *See how you've killed your own mother?*

The next morning, my daughter came into the kitchen and cooked herself a bagel in the toaster. She was wearing cute white Capri's, and her long hair was gathered in a perfect ponytail. I, on the other hand, looked five-hundred years old, and was wearing mismatched pajamas.

I told her I was sorry for my bad behavior, and suggested we start anew. My new parenting strategy, which I had devised around four in the morning, was to teach by example. I would be the first to apologize, the first to rise above. The expression "kill her with kindness" popped into my head, but I was too close to the edge to feel comfortable with that language.

"It wasn't my fault," my daughter responded to my apology, but at least she didn't take her plate into another room to avoid my company.

When the girls left the house that morning for school, I had to chase the older one down the walkway to kiss her goodbye, still wearing my mismatched pajamas. She allowed one quick hug, but there was no "I love you," like she sometimes tossed over her shoulder.

I was an embarrassment—it hit me, as I watched my husband drive away with our daughters. Every morning, he chauffeured them to school on the way to his office—the perfect family of three. I was the outsider, like one of those visiting relatives that kids have to endure; the weird aunt who always has fuchsia lipstick on her teeth, is clueless about everything, and pollutes your sheets with her old-person's skin. I didn't wear fuchsia lipstick, but I was something to be endured all the same, me and my ridiculous pajamas.

The rest of the day, I couldn't concentrate. I tried to work in my home office ("You're *always* working," according to my daughters), but I kept getting up from my desk, wandering around the house, carrying on upsetting conversations in my head. I was a horrible mother, a stupid idiot. Stupid! Stupid! Stupid! In our house, we also have a rule about calling people stupid, but how else would you describe a mother who came *this* close to faking a heart attack, just so her kid could discover her dead?

But then I would get angry all over again. Hormones or no hormones, there was no excuse for my daughter's behavior. How dare she be so rude to me? I was her mother. She needed to show me some respect. In the kitchen, I made myself a sandwich, slathering on the mayonnaise. I was sick of catering to her moods. Sick of feeling rejected. Sick of being told what I could and could not do.

"Tween," I yelled, even though there was no one in the house. "Tween! Tween! Tween!"

I needed to get a grip. I needed another parenting strategy. From now on, I decided, my daughter and I would simply cohabitate. We would live in the same house, under the same roof, but she would do her thing, and I would do mine. No more trying to connect, no more reaching out. She could stop feeling embarrassed and disgusted. I could stop feeling mad and hurt. Her father could raise her, and I wouldn't take it personally one bit.

At 3:15, the school bus arrived at the end of our street. I watched out the kitchen window as my daughter trudged up the driveway, her slim body bent from the weight of her overstuffed backpack. I knew why it was so heavy. It was full of homework she only allowed her dad to check, and books she refused to share with me, even though we both love to read.

Her footsteps sounded on the porch. Quickly, I reviewed my options. If she was in another one of her moods, I could tell her that her behavior was unacceptable. If she said something hurtful, I could go to my desk and pretend to work. I could scream and cry, in the hopes of making a lasting impression, or I could run upstairs to my room, and not make the mistake of coming out.

She came into the house and dropped her heavy backpack in the middle of the floor.

I went over to her and hugged her. This time she hugged me back, a real hug that clarified everything. "There's my girl," I smoothed the top of her perfect ponytail. There's my sweet, sweet girl.

"I'm starving," she announced good-naturedly, and headed to the kitchen.

I watched her go, relieved to see her happy, grateful to have her back. The hormones, no doubt, would return in the near future to wreak more emotional havoc. When they did, I could choose from a whole list of parenting strategies, and likely would need every one of them. But the one thing I knew for sure, the one thing that I didn't have to learn as a parent because it just was and would always be, was that I could never, never not love this girl. She was a tween. But I was her mother.

But Enough about Me

As bad luck would have it, the hostess of this luncheon for women in the arts had seated me next to an elegant woman with silvery blond hair smoothed back with a tortoise-shell headband. Worn on young girls, the tortoiseshell headband might simply suggest an over-controlling mother who wants her daughter to be perfect in every way. But on women of a certain age, this accessory delivers a clear message: *I am a woman of considerable means. Do not presume we are equals. If we did not live in America, where any acknowledgment of class or aristocracy is frowned upon, we would neither move in the same circles, nor occupy this same table as we are now.*

I tucked my purse and gym bag under my chair. A quick glance around the private dining room revealed other harbingers of my being outclassed — pearl chokers, linen dresses, pocketbooks with clasps. But unlike the tortoiseshell headband, those items didn't come with parallel rows of sharp little teeth.

"Hello, I'm Marion." Lady Headband paused her conversation with the woman to her right. She extended a creamy hand with prominent blue veins.

"And I'm Amanda." The woman beside her — hair coiffed liked a Roman helmet, narrow-framed glasses — offered a polite smile. Replace the smile with a contemptuous look and Amanda reminded me of the lady who had put me in my place when I was at the library last week. My flip-flops had been propped on a low table while I typed on my laptop.

"That's a beautiful piece of furniture," the woman had peered down at my feet over her rims. "*Very* expensive."

It could be the same woman, I thought but then again I could just be paranoid.

Ours was a round table for eight; its circumference too big to reach across the expanse of white linen and shake hands with everybody. I was the last to arrive, save for the person assigned the seat to my left. The place card for the missing guest read "Beverly," also the name of my mother-in-law, but given her predilection for clipping coupons, I doubted this was her.

It appeared I was also the youngster in our group. The woman directly across from me must have been close to one hundred, her pallor reanimated with a shaky hand— scribbled brows, a smear of dark pink liplines, two uneven spots of rouge. I wished I was sitting next to her. I like talking to really old people.

The server appeared, offering a choice of drinks. By the time I'd decided on a cranberry spritzer, the other ladies at my table had resumed their conversations. Eavesdropping, I learned Marion and Amanda had both recently traveled to Japan. Apparently, the Pure Water Temple of Kyoto was beautiful, and worth fighting the crowds.

I looked around the dining room, estimating about fifty women in attendance. I had assumed I would know a few people here, given that many of my friends are writers or artists of some kind. Like me, they aren't the type to turn down a free lunch, or better yet a free luncheon, which implies fare of a higher social status. The only person I recognized, however, was our hostess who wasn't even my friend—she was my landlady. I rented a small space to teach writing workshops in one of the many buildings she owns.

Suddenly, I caught on. These people were not women in the arts, not like me anyway, spending the morning at the computer, eking out a few paragraphs of prose, grabbing a shower at the last minute, trying to find something presentable to wear, realizing, too late, that the ruffle on this silk blouse looked like a baby's bib, wondering what it would it hurt to put a little wine in a travel mug for the fifteen minute ride to the restaurant, deciding against it, and promising myself (again) that I would go to my exercise class right after this luncheon because I had already paid for it and I knew I would never do push-ups and sit-ups on my own because I was a lazy slob and a bad writer and in serious need of some endorphins.

These women, I realized, were *patrons* of the arts. It all made sense now: our philanthropic hostess; the predominance of older, well-appointed guests; the location of this restaurant, not in my economically diverse town, but one upscale town over. Most of the women who lived in this community were not only wealthy, but possessed a daunting degree of civic duty and global responsibility. During elections, for example, they didn't just display campaign signs; they retrieved those signs post election, and turned them into book bags for needy children in Honduras.

"Excuse me." The server reached over my shoulder to deliver a basket of hard-crusted rolls.

Good, something to occupy my hands. I took a roll, cracking it in half. With tiny, silver tongs, I retrieved two balls of butter from a chilled bowl. By now it was painfully obvious to me that my seatmate to the left, Beverly, was a No Show. This situation happened to me with peculiar frequency, at wedding receptions, dinner parties, and most recently at a conference of four hundred humor writers. Every assigned table in the Marriott's Banquet Room in Dayton, Ohio was filled with the exception of mine, occupied solely by me and a massive man with a walking aid who no doubt would have switched seats, if his gout-riddled feet had allowed mobility. Despite the focus of the conference, I failed to see the humor in this situation.

With no Beverly to turn to, this left me overly dependent on Marion, who was still chatting away with Amanda. What, I wondered, could be so fascinating about Japan? Actually I knew the answer to that question, not because I had been there, but because I had recently attended a reading by a novelist who wrote about Japanese women employed as table-tops. Apparently, people pay big money to eat sushi off their naked bodies. I learned that this is a long-standing Japanese practice called *Nyotaimori*, which some people consider degrading to women, while others view it as a healthy sexual fetish. Marion and Amanda could know all this, if they bothered to include me in their conversation. So could my other seatmates for that matter, except our over-large table didn't facilitate easy conversation.

Yes, I said sushi, I imagined myself repeating loudly for the benefit of the centenarian across from me, *right off their naked bodies.*

The server returned, bearing a large tray of bowls above her head.

"What kind of soup is this?" I inquired.

"Chilled asparagus with crème fraiche. It's one of our most popular items."

"It certainly is an astonishing shade of green."

"Fresh cracked pepper?" she asked.

"Oh yes." If only she would stay and talk with me the entire luncheon.

"Enjoy." She glided away, a single bowl remaining on her otherwise empty tray—the fucking No Show's.

As always when surrounded by people of refinement,

I found myself affecting their mannerisms. Already, I had used the word "astonishing," which normally doesn't roll off my tongue. Now I made a point to spoon my soup away from me, tilting it sideways into my mouth.

Plop.

A dollop of green foam landed on the ruffle of my silk blouse. I wiped at it with my napkin, smearing it down the light fabric. In general, I am not a clumsy person, with the exception of spilling food down my front when I am trying to look nice. Likely this is rooted in some deep-seated psychological issue: maybe I'm projecting my social anxiety onto my wardrobe, or trying to deflect attention to a flaw not part of my actual person. At the moment, however, I preferred to blame good manners, or more specifically, Marion and her tortoiseshell headband, for the stain on my blouse. This never would have happened if she wasn't ignoring me.

"How do you know our hostess?" I asked, fixing her with a missile lock-on gaze.

She looked up, her soup spoon midway to her mouth. "Our husbands are law partners," she said. "We're starting a scholarship program for young artists."

Always the young artists, I thought. Why doesn't anyone care about middle-aged artists?

"Oh really," I said, and then I couldn't think of another thing to say or ask about her scholarship program, try as I might. Looking at her face, a smooth mask of pressed powder, all I could think of was how I needed to start saving for a facelift. An awkward silence followed, or at least it felt awkward to me, given my discomfort with even slight lapses in conversation. I sensed I would soon lose Marion, if I didn't do something fast.

"I'm a writer," I announced. This came out the way a four-year-old might say, "I'm a big girl."

"What do you write?" Marion inquired. This was a perfectly reasonable response, no different from when somebody introduces herself as a teacher, which elicits the natural follow-up, "What do you teach?" Or when someone claims to be a prisoner, prompting the obvious, "What did you do?" Still, I usually dread this question because whatever confidence I am feeling in my career at that moment is almost always dashed when it becomes clear the person has never heard of me or read any of my work.

"Well, I created a book series that invited hundreds of women across the country to record what they were doing and thinking and feeling on a single day."

"What an interesting idea," Marion gracefully sipped from her spoon.

Yes, it was an interesting idea, I thought, but I wasn't entirely convinced of her sincerity. I felt compelled to prove myself to her.

"The women in the project came from all walks of life," I elaborated. "Celebrities, funeral directors, nuns, mothers with twelve children. . . ." Then, like a geyser, my words kept erupting, until I had detailed every trial and triumph over the six years and fifteen hundred participants it took to complete the three volumes in the book series.

This happens sometimes when I'm feeling awkward or insecure, or even when I'm just being my normal self. I start talking and can't seem to stop, even though I can hear myself going on and on. Sometimes before leaving my house, I'll ink the word *hush* in tiny letters on the crook of my hand, in the hope that this will remind me to shut up. Today, unfortunately, my hands were unmarked, except for some chipped, mauve nail polish.

"I also run a Writer's Center," I continued with my résumé. "It's just one room with orange walls and comfy furniture, but we've seen some fabulous writing come out of it. In fact, I wrote a book for writers . . ."

I have been in the position Marion found herself in now, held hostage by the nonstop talker. First, you are transfixed by the torrent of words, the cluelessness, the solipsism of the speaker. Then you begin to attend to small, previously overlooked details: the number of times she blinks per minute, the pull of her earrings on her earlobes, how that dark freckle on her chest is shaped like Oklahoma. Eventually, her words blur together. You continue to feign attention, but your mind wanders: Do my bottom teeth show when I talk? Is that ceiling fan powerful enough to decapitate someone? Finally, you grow angry, first at yourself: *Why am I still listening to this person?* Then at the speaker, *Will you just shut the hell up!* You know you should say something, do something, but by this point you don't trust your own judgment. *Did I actually make that hanging motion, or just think it?*

The soup has given way to herb-encrusted salmon and warm goat cheese salad. When the server brought my plate, this time I barely acknowledged her, partly because I was too busy talking, partly because I had appropriated more airs. Here was a member of the invisible working class, from which I was trying desperately to distinguish myself.

"Did you know Louise is a new grandmother?" Marion abruptly changed the subject.

No, I did not know Louise is a new grandmother, I thought, feeling rebuffed. In fact, I didn't even know Louise, not that this mattered because Marion had turned her attention back to Amanda. "The baby's name is Harrison," she added. "Louise told me she practically has to pry him out of his mother's hands just to get a chance to hold him."

"I knew Amy and Stu have been trying for years," Amanda said.

I ate my salmon while the two women gossiped. Louise. Amy. Stu. Baby Harrison. Whoever these people were, they clearly had no use for me.

"Louise calls Harrison her miracle grandbaby," Marion added. Ah, an opening.

"Last year I helped a doctor write a book about women who can't have sex," I piped up, thinking this was a good opportunity to sound in on the topic of miracle babies, and show that I was a serious writer. "These women want to have intercourse, but they have this little-known condition called vaginismus..."

It's funny how particular words in certain social settings seem to project at a higher acoustic intensity, vaginismus being the perfect example. As soon as the word left my mouth, it seemed to catch the ear of my seatmates across the table, none of whom had been paying any attention to me before.

"The incidence rate is actually quite high." I decided to forge ahead because, really, what choice did I have? Once a train has derailed, you just have to ride it out. "In fact, vaginismus is as common as erectile dysfunction!"

The old woman across the table raised her scribbled eyebrows.

"Fortunately," I reassured her, "with new treatment options, there is a cure."

Our hostess, thank goodness, chose that moment to tap a hand-held microphone. All chairs turned to face her standing at her table. How had I gotten myself into this mess? I thought. All I had wanted to do was to convince Marion and the others that I was a somebody, yet somehow I had ended up talking about erectile dysfunction.

The hostess gave a short speech, thanking us for our contribution to the arts. "Through your individual and collective efforts, you have made our community a better place to create, to work, and to live." She raised her glass. We followed suit in a toast to ourselves. While it should have been obvious all along, I understood now that I had not been invited to this luncheon because I was a writer, a realm in which I constantly sought validation, but because I was a writing teacher who rented a single room with orange walls.

Chairs scraped again and we turned our attention to dessert. I vowed to focus on my Crème Brule and make only short, appropriate remarks. Or maybe just keep my mouth shut altogether.

Someone at the table raised the topic of quilts, specifically quilts that could be donated for a silent auction to raise money for an after-school arts program. Quilts were an easy subject for me to remain silent, having grown up in Amish farm country. Since childhood, I have associated quilts with the smell of manure, and no amount of craftsmanship can change that.

"Any other fund-raising ideas?" Amanda raised the question.

"How about a bake sale?"

"Or we could do a community spelling bee."

My experience with fund-raising was nil, given I avoided committee work like the plague. But then I realized I did have a suggestion, a good one, and best of all it involved my best celebrity author story. Here was a chance to redeem myself and name drop at the same time.

"A few years ago," I started, "I was invited to participate in a library fundraiser in Florida. Patrons of the library organized dinner parties where donors could mingle with well known writers . . ."

Marion touched my arm lightly.

"Excuse me," she placed her napkin on the table. "I'm afraid I need to run to another appointment." As if on cue, the others quickly followed suit. One of the women made a point to help our hundred-year-old seatmate from her chair, lest her infirmity inhibit her escape. In what seemed like seconds, the table was cleared.

But wait! Wait! I wanted to cry out. I hadn't even gotten to the good part of my story, the part about Khaled Hosseini, the bestselling author of *The Kite Runner.* Khaled and I had been assigned to the same dinner party for the fund-raiser. After we had mingled with donors, we wandered to the far side of the swimming pool to smoke and chat. *Who would have thought,* I would have smiled with self-deprecation, *me bumming a cigarette from Khaled Hosseini. And I don't even smoke!*

If Marion had stuck around, she would have found this last comment amusing. Then I would have assured her that Khaled was as good looking in person as he is on his book jackets. He was also very nice and we got along well, and even stayed in touch for a while after the event. *We're not super good friends*, I would have confessed, given that he had probably forgotten me by now, *but I do have his private home number.*

But I never got the chance to say any of this because the luncheon was over. My table was deserted, with no one left to impress but me and the fucking No Show.

I gathered my purse and gym bag, and then headed to the ladies' room to change for the gym. If I hurried, I could still make it to my exercise class just two blocks away. I was half changed when I realized I had forgotten to bring a tee-shirt and packed only one sneaker. Oh well. I would go anyway, clearly in need of endorphins now more than ever.

Outside the restaurant, a woman called my name. "Yes?" Her face was vaguely familiar, though I had no idea who she was.

"I went to your reading at the bookstore last month," she

said. "I just wanted to say how much I enjoy your work."

"Thank you," I said. "Really, thank you." This was exactly the kind of attention I lived for, a total stranger stopping me in the street to say how much she appreciated my writing. But not now, I thought. Not when I was wearing a stained bib with calf-length sweatpants and strappy sandals.

She headed off in the opposite direction, while I continued to totter my way to my exercise class. So that was that, I thought. My one and only fan would forever assume I dressed like a crazy person. Meanwhile Marion didn't even know my Khaled Hosseini story. But of course now Marion had an author story of her own.

The other day I was at a luncheon for women in the arts, I could just hear her saying this to her friends, all of them wearing tortoiseshell headbands. *There was this dreadful writer seated next to me with soup spilled down her front.* Here, Marion would dismiss me with a wave of her blue-blooded hand. *I really can't remember her name, but what I do remember is that she just went on and on about some kind of sexual dysfunction . . .*

THE SECRET

Several years ago a book came out called *The Secret* and, thanks to Oprah, it went straight to the number one spot on the *New York Times* bestseller list. Then it went on to spawn DVDs, sequels, and cults. The book is about something called the Law of Attraction, and the secret is that you can get whatever you want—from fame to fortune to a passing grade in Algebra II—by following three required steps: ask; believe; receive. According to the book's author, Rhonda Byrne, folks like the Buddha, Beethoven, and the creator of the *Chicken Soup for the Soul* series all knew the secret. That's how the Buddha got to be the Buddha, explains Rhonda, a former television producer from Australia; that's why a book like *Chicken Soup for the Golfer's Soul* can become an international bestseller.

For most of my life I didn't know the secret. In fact, I didn't even know there was a secret until the book came out, and even then I might have overlooked this news, given that my taste in reading doesn't usually run toward self-help. But the publisher of *The Secret* is the same boutique publishing house that acquired my first book, so I grew curious. How can one of the publisher's titles (not mine) be the fastest-selling book of all time, and another title (mine) be the opposite, or at least feel that way? I suspect this discrepancy might have something to do with the fact that my book has a lot of pages, while Rhonda Byrne's text—as sleek and compact as a pocket pet—is not only a fast read, but promises the key to obtaining health, wealth, and wisdom. But that's just a wild guess.

Thankfully, even before reading *The Secret*, I did know enough to do some things to attract good fortune, or at least ward off the Evil Eye. For example, after I complete my bi-weekly jog down a stretch of Route 14 and back, I always tap my mailbox three times while I am still gasping for breath.

Tap. Tap. Tap.

One time I forgot to do this, so I trudged back up our steep driveway and tapped the mailbox six times.

Tap. Tap. Tap. Tap. Tap. Tap.

I even considered backtracking down our street and jogging toward the mailbox again, because retro-tapping isn't the same as tapping immediately after the last step of a grueling 2.9-mile run. But by then I was too exhausted to carry through with this idea, and I'm not really that superstitious anyway. Knock on wood.

I've also made a point not to indulge in self-defeating behavior, a lesson ingrained in me since childhood, after years of hearing my mother's refrain, "If you don't stop that crying, I'll give you something to cry about." Ever mindful, even all these years later, I try not to throw tantrums in public, even when people make me do things I don't want to do, like earn a living or recycle, or when the barista at my coffee shop forgets to substitute soy in my latte, despite my lengthy explanation about how I am seriously lactose intolerant. I also make a point to get out of bed most mornings. I bathe on a semi-regular basis. I practice pronouncing words like "gravitas" and "arugula" so that I can drop them into conversations. I do these things because I know that not doing them could be perceived as self-defeating, and I want to come across as a winner!

But now, thanks to *The Secret*, I realize that compulsive tapping and passable hygiene are not enough, or at least not enough to attract all the things that I want out of life,

specifically easy money, and an online affair with that lanky
Latino guy who said hello to me once at the bagel shop in
an accent that made me forget that I'm almost old enough
to be his mother. You have to *think* positive, Rhonda Byrne
asserts; you have to really *believe* that you are going to get
that check in the mail without lifting a finger; you have
to truly convince yourself that the date on your birth cer-
tificate couldn't possibly be so long ago that you actually
owned a Peter Frampton poster and hung it in your college
dorm room.

Most people (not my husband or children, of course)
actually see me as a positive person. If someone comes up
to me and asks, "Do you think I could be a Navy SEAL?"
I'm likely to respond, "Sure, if that's what you want, go
for it!" My philosophy — at least when it comes to other
people — is the same as the message on the voicemail of that
effeminate figure skater in the movie *Blades of Glory* — "If
you can dream it, you can do it." I have no problem believing
that everybody else can achieve their dreams, even if that
somebody is middle-aged and has bad knees. But when it
comes to feeling positive about my own aspirations, let's just
say that my internal monologue is a screed of negativity — *I'll
never get another book contract . . . I'm never going to write
a bestseller . . . I'll never make this light . . .*

In *The Secret*, Rhonda explains that this kind of negativity
doesn't just bring you (and everybody else around you) down;
it also can work like magical thinking, actually *causing* bad
things to happen, including very, very, *very* bad things.
Terminal disease! Poverty! Widespread disaster! Apparently,
the energy you put into the world is exactly what comes back
to you. Like attracts like, is how Rhonda puts it, so even
fleeting negative thoughts — a.k.a. "incorrect thinking" — can
spell big trouble.

As soon as I learned this, I couldn't help but wonder how far back to apply this "like-attracts-like" concept. Was the Law of Attraction relevant to my childhood, for example? God forbid, did that explain why Benny Mundorf, a former classmate of mine, had a crush on me from first through fifth grade? Benny Mundorf inexplicably had lime-green pee, and clearly didn't care who knew it since he never flushed the toilet in the class bathroom. Was I *like* Benny Mundorf, if not in the color of my urine, than in other, equally unpleasant ways? Was that why he was attracted to me?

And if the Law of Attraction applies as far back as child-hood, I wondered, who's to say it doesn't transcend lifetimes? Who's to say it doesn't affect the very circumstances and geography of our birth? Are there souls, right now, floating around in the ether, waiting to be reconstituted, who have yet to learn the secret? *Yeah, like I'm going to be the next Bill Gates*, thinks one uninformed sad-sack of a soul who never bothered to watch Oprah. Then boof! Off his spirit goes, implanted in the womb of some poor woman in Darfur, a country devastated by war, drought, genocide, and apparently a lot of negative thinking.

In *The Secret*, Rhonda also stresses the importance of visualization. You need to make it your intention to look for and admire what you want, thus summoning that positive energy to you. Just as importantly, you need to *avoid* visualizing what you don't want, she instructs. And if you do see something negative? Refocus your mind's eye immediately on a more pleasant image! Say you're trying to lose a few pounds. *If you see people who are overweight*, writes Rhonda, *do not observe them, but immediately switch your mind to the picture of you in your perfect body and feel it.* Applying this concept more broadly, I presume the same advice holds for sick people — don't look at them!

If negative images beget negative outcomes, then clearly cancer is contagious.

Ask. Believe. Receive. I hear you Rhonda, just like the millions of other book buyers and DVD owners who want in on the secret; just like Oprah and the Buddha who — call me crazy — I'm beginning to believe may be one and the same. I want to be a positive person. I want to attract fame and fortune. I want a cushy life, now and for many lifetimes to come. I'm not just asking, Rhonda, I'm begging — "Please don't send my soul to Darfur. Please don't send my soul to Darfur." But now, thanks to *The Secret*, I understand that my pleading may not be enough. In fact, I suspect I'm in big trouble. Because now that I'm thinking about war, drought, and genocide, it's just too hard to erase those negative images

WATER, WATER EVERYWHERE

Saturday started off with pouring rain and the downstairs toilet not flushing. Just what I need, I thought, or maybe I yelled it at my husband and kids. Luckily, toilets — and basically everything related to household maintenance — are not my problem. They're my husband's purview, so the flushing problem could have been a minor inconvenience (after all, our other two toilets seemed to be working just fine) except for the fact that it put my husband in a bad mood.

"This house if falling apart." Steve swatted aside the little wicker basket of potpourri and wrenched off the lid to the toilet tank. Where had I heard that before? I thought, as I volumized my lashes with Maybelline Thick Lash. As usual, Steve was catastrophizing. Probably all that was needed was to do something with that little ball and chain thingy in the tank that I refused to touch, let alone learn how to re-attach, but Steve tends to over-react about all things septic. According to him, our waste disposal challenges were beyond dire at this point, and boiled down to two choices. One: have the septic system drained every month to buy us time before a shit-storm obliterates our front yard. Or, two: come up with a million dollars to buy a brand new septic system.

"A million dollars?" I rolled my eyes, careful not to smudge my mascara. Whatever. I had more important things on my mind. That morning, I had to take my first CPR class at Curves where I worked part-time, then hightail it to a memorial service for the wife of a photographer I sometimes worked with, then hustle home to make Chicken Athena for six.

Steve and I were having friends over for dinner, and I didn't want to rush the meal preparation. Working with filo dough makes me tense.

I arrived for the CPR training seventeen minutes late, hardly my fault given the torrential downpour outside, and all those nothing-better-to-do drivers who refused to go over the speed limit. I knelt next to the one unclaimed body lying face-up on the Curves gym floor. Two other newly hired fitness technicians, as well as my boss, Dixie, were already stationed by their plastic torsos. Dixie gave me the hairy eyeball as I started finger-combing my rain-flattened hair.

"Sorry I'm late," I stage-whispered, though, in truth, I wasn't the least bit sorry. Dixie was the reason I was stuck here in the first place, after having successfully avoided CPR training my whole life, on the theory that if I knew how to revive a choking victim with vomit pooled in his mouth, then fate would most likely put me in a position where I'd encounter one.

Yet here I was on a Saturday morning, fulfilling a requirement passed down by Curves' corporate that all of the employees at all of its franchises must be certified in CPR. When Dixie first mentioned this requirement to me during my job interview, I'd brushed it aside, just like I'd brushed aside all the rumors that the Texas-based company was run by right-wing nut-jobs who channeled corporate funds to support extremists like abortion clinic bombers and homeschoolers. I'd only applied for this part-time job so that I could use the exercise machines for free and tone up among ladies who were most likely older and fatter than I. That alone, I figured, would provide a much-needed boost to my self-esteem, though my theory hadn't actually panned out. As it turns out, I fit the Curves target demographic perfectly, a depressing thought in and of itself.

Dixie had hired a Viking to teach us CPR, a Viking named
Vince, or at least that was the name stitched onto the breast
pocket of his white bowling shirt with an EMT iron-on patch
on the sleeve. With his white-blond crew-cut and brawny
build, Vince looked equally capable of single-handedly right-
ing an overturned car, and/or barbequing thousands of pounds
of chicken legs and thighs at the Minnesota State Fair.

"First, shake or tap the victim to see if he's responding,
then feel for a heartbeat," Vince held two beefy fingers to
his dummy's neck and waited for a pulse. When, apparently,
there wasn't one, he continued, "If the person is unresponsive,
call 911 before you begin administering CPR."

Dixie and the other technicians listened with composure,
as if Vince was simply offering instructions on how to boot
up a computer. But already I was starting to feel a familiar
panic. Since childhood, I've had a recurring nightmare in
which I am trying desperately to make a phone call but can't
get through, either because the phone is defective or because
my hands are shaking so badly. Sometimes I'm trying to
phone the police because a zombie or a murderer is after
me, but usually I'm just trying to reach my mother, who has
instructed me—in the nightmare, as in real life—"Make sure
to call when you get there!" I know that if I don't manage to
phone home, my mother will be worried sick, which means
that she is going to be livid later when she sees me alive,
and likely embarrass me by yelling in front of my friends.

"A, B, C, D ," Vince started reciting the alphabet, each
letter accompanied by a sharp thrust with the heel of his
hand between his dummy's painted-on nipples. "J, K, L, M,
N, OFF!" I envisioned the poor victim's ribs snapping like
potato sticks. "If the chest does not rise at this point," Vince
paused for dramatic effect. We all stared, eyes glued to his
dummy's chest, hoping to see some movement. "then tilt the

person's head back and give him two breaths." He blew into the sanitized plastic lips inserted into his dummy's mouth hole. "Now you try," he instructed the rest of us.

The others went at it with gusto, rears pointing skyward, their Curves-developed biceps flexing with the effort—fifteen chest compressions, two breaths; fifteen chest compressions, two breaths. Reluctantly, I followed suit, resigned to becoming a lifesaver. As I blew into my own dummy's plastic mouth hole, I imagined him as my Latino heartthrob from the bagel shop in town. He would be so grateful after I saved his life that he wouldn't even notice our twenty-year age difference.

The CPR class ended forty-five minutes late because everyone (everyone but me, that is) voted to tag on infant CPR training. "Yeah, like Curves gets a lot of babies having heart attacks after their workout," I cracked, but Dixie is humorless when it comes to liability.

By the time Vince wrapped things up, I had five minutes to get to the memorial service and the rain just wouldn't let up. On the drive over, I dry-swallowed three Advils. When I checked my face in the visor mirror, I noticed my eyebrows needed plucking. At that point, I almost bagged the service, but I'd already put so much effort into getting this far, it seemed wrong not to show up and get credit for going. I had barely known Ginny, the deceased, though I saw her occasionally when her husband, Paul, and I met for work at their house, or he brought her along to client meetings. She never said much, but she did take copious notes.

The service was located in a big community room in the town hall building. When I got there, a dozen or so other latecomers were still filing into the room. To my relief, Paul was nowhere to be seen so I didn't have to deal with that awkwardness, at least not yet. What are you supposed to say in a situation like this? "I'm sorry?" "How's work?"

"I'll miss Ginny's copious note-taking?" Everything seemed so trite, and of course grief-stricken people can be so touchy. You just never know what's going to set them off.

The room was chock-a-block full of people sitting on metal chairs crammed together in close rows. The stragglers in front of me took forever to claim the few empty seats scattered throughout the crowd. Everyone was being so damn solicitous, not like at regular town meetings in this very same hall, where neighbors yelled at each other over zoning permits and who was going to pay for the new dog park. I waited impatiently as they chattered.

"Oh, there's a space near the front, why don't you take it?"

"Oh no, you go ahead. You were here first . . ."

"Is someone sitting here? Do you mind if I move this umbrella?"

"Bill! So good to see you. How about this rain . . ." Oh, for goodness sakes, just sit down and shut up, I thought. It was bad enough that people came late to a memorial service (at least I had a good excuse; I was saving babies!) but now they were holding things up even further by talking about the weather. I decided to forego any seat and propped myself against a wall near the back of the room. That way, if the service ran late, I could sneak out without being noticed.

The walls of the community room were covered with striking blow-up photographs of Ginny and her family, displayed to major emotional effect. In the pictures Ginny looked vibrant, even beautiful—posing on a mountaintop; beaming next to their daughter at the girl's high school graduation; relaxing on a porch swing with their Persian cat on her lap. I didn't recall Ginny being particularly good-looking in real life, or their cat being all that friendly. It must be nice to have a professional photographer as a husband, I thought with a stab of jealousy. If Steve displayed photos of me at my funeral, the guests would think that I died of red eye.

The service started thirty-five minutes late and, right off the bat, the woman minister got on my nerves. She had one of those clergy-cultivated voices, like she'd just hung up the phone with God and had been personally reassured that everything was under control. She also milked the "power pause" for everything it was worth, trying to make every utterance, however mundane, come across as poetic and pro-found. "Welcome (power pause) to this celebration of a life. . . . Please (power pause) turn off your cell phones. Ginny (power pause) was a bright light . . ."

To pass the time, I scoped out the crowd. A few guests were fanning themselves with their programs. The room did feel stuffy but, really, I couldn't imagine treating a program to a memorial service like a playbill to bad regional theater. There, on the cover, was a perfectly retouched photo of Ginny. And what if Ginny herself, not just her picture, was actually in this room with us? I didn't exactly believe in ghosts, but I did know that if I had recently died, and saw a bunch of my so-called friends using my face as a fan at my memorial service, I wouldn't take it too kindly. In fact, those would be the first people I'd come back to haunt, just to scare the bejesus out of them.

Here is the upside of a memorial service: it really makes you appreciate your own loved ones. A lot of people had an arm draped across the shoulder of the person next to them or were holding hands, including two women sitting directly across from me. In fact, I suddenly noticed, several women in the nearby rows were clearly together. Was I standing in the lesbian seating section? You'd think I would have noticed this sooner, given all the mannish haircuts and clogs. But this is Vermont; who can tell?

Then it occurred to me—I have very few lesbian friends. This seemed a shame, since grieving lesbians make a nice statement at a memorial service, showing the world that you were an accepting, even hip person. I did have a lesbian enemy, I realized, noticing the owner of the local bookstore with her partner at the far end of the row. When my last book came out, I emailed her asking if I could do a reading at her store, but she never responded. Who needs me, I thought with resentment, when Jodi Picoult lives up the street?

Eventually, the minister finished her remarks and recited a prayer—"Our father (power pause) who art in heaven . . ." Next came the remembrances from several of Ginny's loved ones. On one point, they all agreed—Ginny had quite the glow. Not only was she a "bright light," as the minister had stated, but she was also referred to as a "brilliant light," a "shining light," and a "luminous presence." Maybe she died of radioactivity, I thought, but that was my aching lower back talking. It felt like I'd been standing forever.

The best speaker was the neighbor lady, who kept her remembrance short and sweet—how Ginny's kitchen always smelled like whatever was baking in her bread machine. Plus, the neighbor lady couldn't stop weeping, which has its own unique power to transfix an audience. The absolute worst speaker was Ginny's meditation teacher, who went on and on about the spiritual significance of a drop of water and how Ginny—similar to a drop of water—was quiet, but had a big impact on people's lives. Then he announced that he was going to lead us all in a guided meditation.

That's when I cut out, drawing some looks from the lesbians, but what was I supposed to do? By now it was late afternoon and my Chicken Athena wasn't going to cook itself. As I tiptoed toward the door, I gave a fake smile to the bookstore owner, just in case I ever published another book.

Seeing her with her partner made me wish Steve had been here to put his arm around me. On the other hand, I was just as glad to be going home to a working toilet.

On the drive home, the rain still hadn't let up, and some of the roads were borderline flooded. Great, I thought. Our septic system was probably overflowing into the next county. I caught a yellow light and raced through it, nearly hydroplaning into another car when I jammed on my brakes. This scared me so much that I pulled into a convenience store parking lot to calm my nerves. I also wanted a bottle of wine.

Between CPR training, the memorial service, and now this near accident, I'd had it with life and death for one day. I bought my Pinot Grigio and set it on the passenger seat, next to the program from the service. There was Ginny's smiling face beaming up at me. Maybe it was just the airbrushing, but she really did seem to have a glow about her. It was as if she was trying to illuminate something, but what? Beneath her photo, the program showed the dates of her birth and death. My God—it still came as a shock—she was only four years older than I when she died. Healthy one day, then sick and gone less than six months later, just like that.

I drove the rest of the way home, white knuckling the steering wheel and in a bad mood. The windshield wipers could barely keep up with the pouring rain. What a pain, I thought, unable to see more than a few feet ahead. If all these drops of water had a spiritual significance, it was totally lost on me.

A CURE FOR AGING VERMONTERS

Apparently, there's a pill on the market that cures both belly fat and stress. I learned this from an ad on television. The commercial featured real people—not paid actors—who had taken the pill with remarkably diverse benefits. One woman said the pill helped her relax. A distinguished-looking man said the pill helped him enjoy more time with his wife and kids. A shapely woman held up a "before" photograph, and shared how the pill had melted away her unsightly pounds and inches. Now she had energy for the things that mattered. Beside her, the woman's husband squeezed her shoulders then smiled at the resulting cleavage. "Whether you want to reduce belly fat or stress," the announcer guaranteed, "this is a feel good pill."

I couldn't remember the last time my husband smiled at my cleavage. So I got my Visa and found the portable phone wedged between the couch cushions. If I called the toll free number in the next twenty minutes, I'd be eligible for fifty free capsules!

If you watch TV like me, one thing you know for sure: nowadays there is a pill (or cream or patch) for everything— wrinkles, high blood pressure, moodiness, erectile dysfunction, dull teeth, hair loss, and, yes, even belly fat and stress. Which begs the question: Why are so many people still feeling and looking so yucky? Later, flipping through the channels, the answer hit me. These are the people who don't watch TV.

I live in Vermont, a state known for its cows and maple syrup, but not for its cable access. A lot of Vermonters couldn't care less what happens to the Desperate Housewives on Wisteria Lane. They pride themselves on not being among the sixty-three million people who voted on American Idol. Parents, in particular, think that television will turn their children into SpongeBobs. "We don't even own a TV," I hear with astounding frequency when I pick up my daughters after school. But what these parents don't know is that now there is a pill on the market that can actually enhance their child's intelligence. For just three easy payments, their kids could be reading above grade level.

The other week I happened to browse through the newspaper. "Vermonters are old and getting older," read the headline. According to Census statistics, "Vermont is aging faster than any other state in the union." But are we really aging faster? I wondered. Or is it just that most Vermonters don't watch enough TV? We don't know about the anti-aging pills, the energy enhancers, or the miracles of Botox that can set back the clock. Later, I was talking about this article with the mom of one of my younger daughter's friends. This woman is in her early forties, and styles her steel gray hair like a helmet. Instead of watching television, her four kids have all learned to knit.

She asked me, "How old are you?" So I told her.

"You are not!" she accused, as if I had just claimed to be a man posing as a woman. "You look like you could be in your late thirties."

"Well it's true," I said, "I kid you not." Then I smiled with the confidence of someone who has cable . . . and who knows just what toothpaste whitens teeth best.

Copy. Paste.

My father is in a hospital ICU unit, transferred by ambulance yesterday morning from his nursing home. I am in my home office 431 miles away, on deadline for a book project. My work task today is a mindless but cumbersome one. I have high-lighted key passages in over five-hundred online submissions for the book I am working on. Now I need to simply copy those highlighted sections and paste them into a database.

Copy. Paste. Copy. Paste.

My sister, who lives just a few miles from my parents, calls me again. Our dad's condition hasn't changed. "He's been intubated. He's on a respirator," she tells me. I go into the kitchen and pour myself another cup of coffee. It is a nice spring day, blindingly sunny by the greenhouse window. My sister also tells me my mom won't go into my dad's hospital room. "She's pacing the hallway."

"Okay." This is familiar territory. In the months immediately following his first stroke six years ago, my dad endured every kind of emergency procedure. "Yes! Resuscitate!" My mother signed papers and more papers to make this clear.

Copy. Paste. Copy. Paste.

Every day, I need to meet a self-imposed quota for data entry; otherwise I will fall behind on my book deadline. I have been going through the submissions in alphabetical order. Today I am working my way through the Ls and Ms. Tomorrow . . . Tomorrow, I suddenly remember, I'll be on a train. I'm going to see my dad who is dying.

Copy. Paste.

Why doesn't she call? I am thinking of my friend Natalie who was supposed to let me know if she can split the cost of personal training. I have already set up the first appointment with the trainer for tomorrow, so I need her to confirm. Otherwise, I will have to cancel because I can't afford it on my own. Wait a minute. I shake my head in disbelief. Why do I keep forgetting?

My mom calls. "They've scheduled Daddy for an MRI," she tells me. "They're going to see if anything is going on."

Going on. This takes me back. The weeks after my dad's first stroke, our family stood vigil by his hospital bed, watching his left side. *There! He wiggled his toe!* But as it turned out, nothing was really going on.

My mom is still talking. "I know what they're going to say to me." More than grief or fear, I hear anger in her voice. This is how she copes, I remind myself. "Those damn doctors are going to want me to pull the plug. I will not murder your father."

Copy. Paste. Copy. Paste.

The room where I am working is on the shady side of the house. I can't seem to get warm, even though I am wearing a hooded sweatshirt. I don't know much about Feng Shui, but I do know my home office shouldn't be facing the trash cans on our porch. Part of me though, thinks this is funny. I light a tea light candle on the corner of my desk. This will cheer things up. Then it occurs to me, I should have lit the candle for my dad.

My dad died on Mother's Day. When my sister called early yesterday morning to tell me how it looked like this was the end, I imagined myself saying this for years to come. *My dad died on Mother's Day.* But yesterday came and went. I opened cards from my daughters. I didn't think of my dad when the girls and I went shopping for shorts and tank-tops.

I didn't think of him when I wolfed down a second piece of pineapple upside down cake. I felt sorry for myself because I had to do data entry on Mother's Day.

Copy. Paste.

I'm almost through the pile of Ls. I should go for a run but I don't have the time. Oh, and I might miss an important phone call.

I stop what I am doing. *Your dad is dying,* I tell myself. *What is your problem?* I make myself think of him, force a memory. One eventually surfaces from the distant past.

It is summer and we are in the backyard of the house where I grew up. My dad's wearing baggy shorts and dark socks. He looks like he always looked before he got sick, like a dad. I am in my bathing suit, impatient to work on my tan. Finally, he has finished mowing the lawn. Now he is giving our Saint Bernard, Alice, a drink from the hose.

"Want to help water the garden?" he asks. I am a teenager; I don't want to help with anything.

"It's what I live for." I spread my beach towel on the grass. As soon as I roll on my stomach, he sprays me with the hose.

"Daddy!"

He is lying on a hospital bed, on life support. Copy. Paste. Copy. Paste.

My computer dings, signaling a new email. I need a break so I open my inbox. The message is spam; the subject line reads: *Can you imagine you are healthy?* What's that supposed to mean? I am healthy. Is this some kind of sign?

Last night, I dreamed a miracle. My dad stood up from his wheelchair, took a few tentative steps, and then he was walking just fine. Everything about him was normal. *I'm not dreaming this,* I told myself in the dream. *I'm really not dreaming this!* I woke myself up crying. The bedside clock read 4:07 a.m.

You hear stories about people knowing, just knowing, the moment someone close to them dies. I had hoped this was a sign. Then I remembered my dad can't die. My mom won't let anybody pull the plug.

Copy. Paste. Copy. Paste.

I am halfway through the pile of M's. This whole process is taking forever. I hate it and just want it to be over.

IDENTITY THEFT

Every New Year's Eve, I type up a list of resolutions to help the Old Me become the New Me. While the list tends to be really long, the upshot is that I resolve to be a perfect person and lose seven pounds. Then the year dawdles and waddles away. Another December 31 arrives. Once again the Old Me, still imperfect, still carting around those seven pounds, recommits to becoming the New Me. And so it goes, year after year, a ritual as comfortable as it is familiar.

One June, my good friend Frances and her ten-year-old son moved in with my family. They were in the process of relocating, our kids were about the same age, and we have a big house with a big mortgage. So this arrangement made perfect sense for a few months or maybe even longer. Frances seemed to think I was doing her a favor, but I viewed our house-sharing more as an opportunity for middle-aged sleepovers, built-in child-care, and anthropological study.

Frances and I are totally different species. While we share certain superficial traits (both white, American, born at the tail-end of the baby boom generation), that's where our similarities end. Whereas I was born over-caffeinated, Frances takes one breath to my three. She makes gratitude lists that get on my nerves. In her room, she designed a pretty little altar with candles and incense and inspirational quotes. Frances works as a healer, practicing the ancient art of Reflexology, which involves touching people's feet. I don't even like touching my own feet, let alone someone else's.

What's more, Frances is gorgeous. And when I say "gorgeous," I am quoting the bearded guy I was flirting with at the local pub who exclaimed, "My God, you're gorgeous," as he leaned over me to address her. In contrast, later that same week I was at my daughter's school. Another parent pointed to my then twelve-year-old girl and said, "Is that your daughter? She's so beautiful. She must look like her father."

The following interaction between Frances and me speaks to our fundamental differences. I am hunched at my writing desk, dressed like a slob. I smell like garlic. A puckered scum of cream drifts on the surface of my cold coffee, thanks to reheating it in the microwave seventy-five times. I am about to gnaw off my knuckles, which is my creative process.

"Love, light, laughter?" Frances asks, dancing into the room. She aims a pretty silver spritzer in my direction. Frances is a walking apothecary of essential oils. She is also one of maybe nine people in the world who actually looks good in form-fitting yoga pants.

"Okay."

She mists the miasma of garlic above my head. The scent of geranium and essence of orange wafts over my keyboard.

Then off she goes, as bright and bouncy as Tinker Bell's light. I take a sip of cold coffee. The cream scum sticks to my upper lip.

Given these differences between Frances and I, the mind boggles that she would even consider stealing my identity. But steal it she did, bit by bit over the months we shared a house.

It started with jogging. When I was in my twenties and living in Philadelphia, I jogged about eight miles a day. This was around the time of Rocky I, and part of my route included running up the art museum steps and then jumping around with my fists in the air. These days, I jog exactly 2.9 miles to the local mini-mart, where I usually have to pee. It's not a long distance; still, it's enough to give me a feeling of smug superiority.

Then one day, out of the blue, Frances announced that she was going to start jogging. And just like that, she ran my 2.9 miles. This was just wrong, a violation. I would never think to steal her yoga, which she teaches part-time, and which she blatantly used to divert my children's affections. Evening after evening, I would catch her and my daughters in the back room, stretching and posing on side-by-side floor mats. So this was how my girls were spending their free time, instead of doing something mother-daughterly with me.

But as it turned out, stealing my jogging and my children were only the beginning. Out of the kindness of my heart, I introduced Frances to my friends — Judy, Anne, Carole, Melissa. "Look," I would point to Frances, "here is the lady to whom I have graciously opened my home. Aren't I a nice person?" Of course, those weren't my exact words, but that was the gist. In return, within my social circle Frances was supposed to remain a friend of a friend, nothing more. If by chance any of them did encounter her when I wasn't around, the conversation was supposed to have gone something like this:

"Aren't you Frances, Joni's housemate? Isn't she the best?!"

"She sure is. Bye."

"Bye."

Then one day the phone rang and it was Judy . . . calling for Frances! They talked for ages, and I can tell you they weren't planning my surprise party. And later, I learned that Carole and Frances had met for tea. Herbal tea! This was so unfair because herbal tea-drinking is one category in which I can't possibly compete, even though I am a very competitive person. And then another major blow. One day I was having lunch with Anne who gushed on and on about how

Frances was a miracle worker. Apparently, ever since Frances
had started working on her feet, her aches and pains were
gone. Plus, Frances had been helping her become gluten free.
All behind my back!

Lest this read like I am over-reacting, I should add here
that Frances also stole my men friends, or at least the single
ones. They would meet her. Taken with her ridiculously lux-
urious hair and ability to let them finish their sentences, they
would ask her out. Whether she actually dated them or not,
at that point they were lost to me. I couldn't possibly phone
them because I knew if they saw our number on their caller
ID, they would get their hopes up that it might be Frances,
and then I would have to endure the disappointment in their
voices when it turned out to be only me.

With each passing month Frances and I lived in the same
house, she continued to abscond with more and more of
my identity.

She signed up for swing dance lessons, even though I
had been saying for years that I was going to learn how to
swing dance.

When I generously allowed her to borrow my library card in
exchange for returning my seriously overdue books, she stole
my meager fame. The librarian, not knowing me personally,
but recognizing my name on the card, congratulated Frances
on my last book!

Frances also stole the biceps I had been hoping to develop,
by going to the gym while I stayed home and ate gluten. She
actually read some spiritual guru's bestseller that I'd told
everyone I had read. And she had the audacity to lose my
seven pounds, which was just spiteful because she didn't
even need to lose weight. In fact, this made her slightly
underweight, something I have always aspired to be. But
the last straw came when I ran into a mutual acquaintance

who mentioned in passing, "Oh, I saw your friend Frances the other day walking down the street. She looked so happy."

I couldn't believe it! This was what people were supposed to be saying about me. In fact, being happy was central to my annual New Year's resolution to become a perfect person. Yet the last time I happened to catch my reflection in the coffee shop's long glass windows, my expression looked like I'd just smelled a dog fart.

Finally, I caught on to what was really happening. Frances hadn't just stolen my identity; she had stolen the New Me. She had become the person I resolved to be at the beginning of every year. Now I understood why the Old Me was feeling so put out. She didn't like seeing her potential fulfilled by somebody else.

A few months ago Frances moved to her own place a couple miles away from our house. Since then, my family and I haven't done much with her room. The corner where she had arranged her little altar with inspirational sayings and prayer beads is now a refuge for dust balls and discarded, empty boxes earmarked for the landfill. She took her yoga mats with her. The smell of geraniums and essence of orange has dissipated.

Living together for almost two years afforded me the opportunity to observe Frances first-hand—her habitat, her eating habits, her social interactions, all so foreign to my own. Time and again, I experienced a form of culture shock as I witnessed how she lived her life, and questioned her about her strange practices:

"You mean you honest-to-goodness don't cook with Teflon?"

"But what do you think about when you're meditating?"

"Seriously, are you going to just let that slide?"

I've read that in any anthropological study, the cultural

distance between the ethnographer and the people being studied is reduced over months and years. This seems to be true in my case as well. Almost as soon as Frances moved out, I missed her and forgave her for stealing my identity. After all, I realized, who wouldn't want to be the New Me? But as it turns out, forgiveness was just one of Frances' traits that had rubbed off on me.

The other day, Frances and her son dropped by for a visit. When she knocked on the front door, it didn't feel right, not right at all.

"Come in, come in," I welcomed them into our home. "You know you don't need to knock." Already the kettle was heating on the stove, and a scented candle flickered on the kitchen table.

Frances and I stretched out on opposite ends of the comfy couch in the kitchen, while her boy and my girls went off to another part of the house to play. We gabbed and looked through catalogs, just like old times. She sipped her tea and I drank my coffee. I felt happy just sitting there, hanging out, hearing our kids' voices in the background. And while neither of us said the words "love, light, laughter," I was thinking them all the same.

GRIEVING MY LEFT FOOT

Denial

One recent summer morning I woke up, went to take my first steps out of bed, and felt like someone had stuck a knife in my left heel. The pain was so piercing I actually collapsed back on the dog burrowed under the covers. I tried again. Tentatively, I put weight on my heel, experiencing the same excrutiating jab. What had happened to my foot?

As the day wore on, the pain in my heel settled into more of a generalized throb, but the next morning, and the next, and the next, the stabbing was back with those first few steps. Apparently, a little swordsman had taken up residence in the floorboards next to my bed.

"Will you please go see a doctor?" Steve said.

"I'm fine. It's nothing." What was a doctor going to tell me, except something I didn't want to hear? Besides, what few random ailments I had suffered in the past had always disappeared on their own. The latest example was my self-diagnosed, deadly stomach tumor, which had miraculously shrunk after I stopped eating so many carbs.

This situation, however, seemed to be growing worse. Over time, the heel pain wasn't just during those first steps, but every time I tried to walk after having been off my feet for a few minutes.

To get anywhere, I had to resort to creative means of ambulation. Sometimes I shuffled. Sometimes I clutched door jambs and armrests to avoid putting any pressure on my heel. If I was in a hurry, I tended to step normally with my right foot, but tiptoe with the left. This gave my gait a bobbing effect, but allowed the best speed-to-pain ratio. Most of the time, I just limped.

A funny thing happens when you limp. Suddenly you notice all these other people who are limping, too. One time I was limping behind a limper and for no apparent reason the woman turned and gave me the Evil Eye. Did she think I was mocking her? I worried about this, especially when I overtook other limpers, given that I tended to be a speed limper, just as I was a speed walker before my foot problem. I would never dream of mocking the infirm, of this I was certain, but then I remembered one of my favorite gags:

"Walk this way," I would motion whomever I was with to follow me. Then I would hunch my shoulder and start lurching across the floor, dragging my foot like Frankenstein's assistant Igor.

With the help of the Internet, I medically diagnosed myself. What I was suffering from was something called plantar fasciitis, one of the most common orthopedic complaints, with symptoms exactly mirroring my own. The plantar fascia, I read, is a thick band of tissue that connects your heel bone to your toes, and supports the arch of your foot. Repeated strain of this ligament causes tiny tears that lead to swelling and pain. Among those at highest risk for developing plantar fasciitis are: 1.) Runners (I have jogged off and on for thirty years) 2.) People who have high arches (yep) and 3.) Men ages forty to seventy.

Ignoring that bit about aging men, I could rationalize that what was really wrong with my heel was a sports injury. I liked the sound of that—a sports injury—which is something that afflicts athletes, rather than people who are just falling apart. In fact, the evening before my heel pain started, I had taken a cardio kickboxing class that required us to jump around on mats in bare feet and hit a punching bag.

Jab! Jab! Cross!

I was new to kickboxing, and the worst in my class, but this seemed like my ideal form of exercise. Before taking this class, the only outlet for my aggression against the many, many people who had wronged me was to scold them in my imagination. But now I could visualize their faces on the punching bag; I could target their vulnerable body parts.

Jab! Jab! Hook! *Take that, and that, and that!*

Even after my foot pain developed, I kept kickboxing, though not without sneakers because going barefoot only exacerbated the problem. The odd thing was, sometimes my foot actually felt better after exercise, at least for a little while. So if I just kept moving around, I figured, my sports injury would heal itself.

Anger

Why me? Why should this have happened to my foot? It wasn't like I was a two-ton Tessie; I was too vain to let myself go. It wasn't like I had bad genes. Over decades of annual physical exams, I had prided myself on being able to mark all those "no" boxes in that scary health history checklist.

"I guess I'm lucky," I would say to the nurse or doctor, handing over my completed form. This lip service was for the benefit of the humility gods who didn't take kindly to people overlooking their good fortune. But secretly, I couldn't help feeling a smug superiority. My body was a genetic algorithm, evolved far beyond those other poor people with columns full of yeses.

Two months after that first agonizing step, with no relief in sight, I finally went to see a doctor. Or to clarify, I went to see a certified nursing assistant at my primary care physician's office, in order to get a referral to a physical therapist, in order to get a referral to a sports medicine doctor, in order to get a referral to a specialist in podiatry. There is something wrong with a country where you have to go through three people to get an appointment with the person who might actually help you.

And another thing! I hated the term plantar fasciitis, which might as well be called old person's disgusting warty toes because, to my mind, that's exactly what it sounded like. What's more, it was nobody's business why I was step- tip-toeing around town. I didn't make a habit of nosing into other people's problems, asking them why they lisped or what happened to their other hand, so why should they keep prying into mine?

One night after kickboxing, I limped into my house. "I'm never going back," I grumbled. Whereas before, exercise had temporarily alleviated the pain, now it only seemed to make matters worse. I knew there was no choice but to quit.

"You sure have been complaining a lot," someone made the comment. Maybe it was my husband, or kids, or all of them. Well if that was how little they cared, then I'd show them.

"How is your foot?" I lived for my family to ask me this question.

"Fine," I would respond tersely, and that would be the most they were going to get out of me.

By the time I'd finally gotten an appointment to see Dr. Podiatry, six months had elapsed since my heel pain first started. In the interim, I had been treated by two different physical therapists and a sports medicine doctor. My feet had been kneaded, torqued, fed electrical impulses, booted, and, most notably, shot up with enough steroids that I was surprised they hadn't ripped themselves off my ankles, developed rampant acne, and gone on a shooting rampage from a clock tower.

Regardless, I was still in acute and chronic pain at the same time. This was what I told Dr. Podiatry, as I dangled my bare feet off his examining table.

"Micro traumas," Dr. Podiatry explained, as he straightened his Santa tie. This gesture only reminded me that my appointment with him had been half a year in the making. It was like getting an audience with the foot Pope. "Your problem," he elaborated, "has been caused by years of micro traumas to your plantar fascia."

Micro traumas my ass, I thought. For one thing, that was an oxymoron if I ever heard one. And for another thing, I think I would have noticed years' worth of traumas. I'm not exactly the type of person who reacts well in a crisis. Dr. Podiatry also told me I'd probably had disgusting warty toes since I was in my twenties.

"So why haven't I been hobbling around for the past couple decades?" I challenged.

"When we're young," he explained, "we recover much faster."

After I scheduled another appointment with Dr. Podiatry—this one to be fitted for orthotics—I decided I needed some perspective. In my bedroom, I have a big jewelry box containing a hodge-podge of belongings: macaroni necklaces given to me by my kids, some Iraqi money sent by a soldier friend stationed in one of Saddam Hussein's bombed-out palaces, a feather from my beloved dead cockatiel . . . From this mix, I dug out my Complaint Free bracelet, a purple plastic band intended for behavior modification.

Back and forth, back and forth; every time I caught myself complaining, I transferred the band from one wrist to the other. The goal was to not have to switch the bracelet for twenty-one consecutive days because, supposedly, that's how long it takes to break a bad habit. The concept of the Complaint Free bracelet started with the minister of a small congregation in Ohio. Since then, he had managed to leverage the idea into Complaint Free seminars, Complaint Free books, even Complaint Free cruises.

If my foot didn't hurt so much I would print myself a tee-shirt, and here is how it would read: All those healthy footed people got to go on a Complaint Free cruise, and all I got was this lousy bracelet.

I snapped the bracelet onto my other wrist.

Bargaining

Please God, make my foot better and I will never do my Igor impersonation again.

The fact that I was praying made me realize how deeply my prolonged foot pain was affecting me. For one thing, I don't believe in God, at least not in the form of someone you can sit across from at the negotiating table. Okay God, let's hash out this deal! Still, in this time of crisis, or at least crisis of confidence (Would I ever be able to enjoy a shower without footwear again?), I seemed to have found religion.

As much as I wanted my foot to heal, I never prayed aloud, not the way people with real faith do. That would have made me feel too self-conscious.

"Please God . . ." I imagined myself kneeling, my hands clasped in supplication.

"Who are you talking to?" This would be my mother's voice,

sounding like it did when I was a fourteen, trying to have a private phone conversation with a boy.

"No one."
"Well tell no one it's time for you to finish your homework."

Please God, make my foot better and I promise I will be a much kinder, less smug person.

At this point, I had been living the life of a cripple for over six months. I know "cripple" is a word now deemed offensive by the general public, and I can easily go along with that for other people. But in my case I didn't feel "physically challenged" or "differently abled." I felt like a clip-clopping nag who should be put out of her misery.

My only pair of shoes that offered a modicum of relief were heavy-soled slip-ons with a Mary Jane strap. They were cute, because why would I own ugly shoes, but hardly meant to accommodate everything from skirts to pajama pants.

"On a scale of one to ten," Dr. Podiatry asked me during my second appointment, "What is your pain level today?"

"Eleven."

"Okay then," he said, "Now hop on this treadmill and let's see how you do."

Before he could fit me for my orthotics, Dr. Podiatry needed to videotape my footfalls to further evaluate my problem. I limped barefoot on the treadmill for a few minutes while he and I watched the big monitor that showed me walking from the back.

Please God, make it true that the camera adds ten pounds.

After I returned to the examining table, Dr. Podiatry sat across from me and explained the situation. I had compensatory

hyperpronation, or too much inward rotation of the foot.
The ideal motion of the foot is neutral pronation. Two degrees
off strains the ligament. Five degrees off results in severe
pain. Seventeen degrees off (me) makes you a plantar fasciitis
time bomb. Because I was "slim and trim," the onset of
symptoms had been delayed. Dr. Podiatry also showed me
X-rays of my feet, revealing heel spurs, or bony outgrowths,
on both my calcaneus bones.

To summarize the most useful information I took away
from this appointment: Dr. Podiatry thought I was slim and
trim!

*Please God, let the custom orthotics I have just ordered work
miracles, and I won't even complain about the $378 price tag.*

Depression

My feet were shattered. My situation was hopeless. Or so it
seemed. A mere seven months ago I was living the dream
of any able-bodied, middle-aged woman who had managed
to convince herself that fifty was the new thirty. But then,
just like that, I had become the star of my own Lifeline
commercial.

"What are you looking for?" Steve asked me one night as
he sat up in bed, rubbing his eyes. It was two in the morning.
I was on my hands and knees on the floor. Naturally, the Light
Sleeper had woken up, even though I had purposely made a
point not to wear my clip-cloppy shoes.

"I'm not looking for anything," I snapped. "I'm crawling
to the bathroom."

While I waited for the arrival of my custom orthotics, a
shroud of defeat settled over me. Inserts for my shoes?

How were two little molded pieces of plastic going to restore me to my former self?

On one level, I understood that millions of people faced greater physical challenges than plantar fasciitis, or even disgusting warty toes. I also realized that, if it was true that God only gave us as much as we could handle, He must have set the bar pretty low for me. Still, after so many years of being able to move around without pain, I felt entitled to good feet, if only because I had always enjoyed them.

Way back when, the physical therapists who first treated me had sent me home with handouts describing all the stretching exercises that were supposed to put a stop to all this nonsense. I had dangled my heels off steps, rolled frozen Pepsi bottles under my arches, and written the alphabet in the air with my feet. But my condition had only worsened, bringing me to the point where the pain in my left heel now had spread to my other foot, up my Achilles tendons, and into my calves. I imagined my body as a storm-tracking map, the dark swirls around my lower extremity rapidly moving in a northerly direction.

I stopped doing physical therapy. I stopped exercising.

I pretty much stopped moving at all.

"I'm home," my children would call from the foyer after returning from their days at school. From my spot on the chaise lounge in the bedroom, I could hear the clunk of backpacks and the kicking off of boots.

"I'm upstairs," I'd call down, my lap covered with a blanket. It was amazing how much colder the long winter seemed when one simply reclined all day.

My body felt like it was petrifying.

Where had I seen this kind of deterioration before? Ah yes, my mother. One Christmas she had come to visit us in Vermont, looking fairly hearty. A week after she returned home she fell down two steps and dislocated her shoulder. It "froze" during the healing process, and the rest of her body quickly followed suit. Within a year, my mom was confined to her recliner, unable to press the channel arrow on her remote control without assistance.

"It was just two steps!" my family decried to her doctors. "It was just a dislocated shoulder. How could this happen so fast?"

"It just does sometimes, when a person gets old."

Acceptance

My orthotics arrived in February, eight months after that first painful step. As long as I inserted them in whatever shoes I was wearing I could walk normally, and even jog without feeling a twinge. Still, the experience made me attuned to other creeping aches and inconveniences—a stiffness in my bones, an inexplicable bruise on my arm, the occasional problem with word retrieval. Here were the nuances of aging I had neither noticed nor previously acknowledged.

If I could not fight the inevitable, I thought, I might as well prepare for it. Or so I tried to tell myself, but acceptance had never been my strong suit. This lacking came into relief when I saw a photograph in the newspaper of a smiling woman who had lost her leg in an accident when she was hit by a car a few years ago. What struck me was how she was in her wheelchair, shoveling her driveway after a winter storm. "I'm game," she was quoted as saying. "I love the snow."

Seeing how this woman remained so positive and full of energy, even in challenging circumstances, all I could think was, *You have got to be kidding*!

Before my foot problems, I honestly could not conceive of

my own death. This isn't to imply that I didn't have moments when I thought I was going to die, say when the car I was driving skidded out of control, or I choked on a lump of cheese fondue. But those were instances of panic at the prospect of horrible suffering, not about the reality that one day I would be gone. Not gone as in off to the store. But gone gone.

Despite the fact I am a writer, I have never enjoyed a good memory. I am bad at recalling people's faces or names. My family has had to remind me of entire vacations. I barely remember my childhood. That's why it has always struck me how clearly I recall the first time I met Steve. I can still see the snowflakes melting on the shoulders of his parka when he walked into the bar. The first words we exchanged remain as clear as dialogue on a page. I can feel my fingers stiffening as we stood outside in the cold, and I wrote my number on a matchbook.

This sort of recall may not be unusual for other people, or perhaps even for me if I had known then what I know now, that this would be the man I would marry over twenty-five years ago. But that night Steve was just another cute guy in a bar; it was just another snowy night in the city. Given my normal state of inattention, this memory imprinted in my mind to serve as a kind of demarcation. Now—this moment—is the beginning of your future.

In a strange way, I believe the same is true about that morning when I first felt the pain in my left foot. Since then, I am sure I have forgotten much worthier memories, yet I can bring back that morning in full sensory detail—sitting up in bed, my foot making contact with the floorboard, the sharp stab in my heel, falling back on the dog.

This moment, too, feels like a demarcation, the beginning of my future as a mere mortal. I know I have held off that reality longer than most people my age, thanks to my smug genes and, no doubt, my preternatural talent for ignoring mini traumas.

Once in a while I will bounce on my heels, just to do a quick check for pain. So far, so good, I reassure myself, but now I can see it and feel it. My body is wearing down. I am not old yet, but I am aging. Yes, my orthotics are two tough pieces of plastic, but even they can't stave off the relentless pressure of time.

HOW TO WRITE MORE,
WRITE BETTER, AND BE HAPPIER

Months had passed since I had accepted an invitation to speak at a conference for writing teachers, and now it had come down to this. I needed to get up at 4 a.m. to figure out what I was going to say. The conference was this morning, and I had to be prepared and presentable in exactly four hours.

Downstairs, I pushed the button on the coffeemaker and sat in front of my computer. *How to Help Students Write More, Write Better, and Be Happier*, I typed. This was the title of the talk I had submitted to the conference organizers, though now I wondered, too late: *Was that heading even grammatically correct?* Given my audience of former English majors, I would find out soon enough.

No point in trying to think without an infusion of caffeine. I drank a couple cups of coffee while checking Facebook, Twitter, and the Amazon ranking for my book on writing that I'd be hawking at the conference. At the moment, my ranking was 294,333, which meant that—of all the books listed on Amazon—294,332 of them were outselling mine. I toyed with the idea of ordering a copy of my own book, which experience has taught me temporarily boosts its ranking by several thousand points, but this was getting costly, not to mention pathetic.

Time to buckle down. Eventually, I typed a sentence. Then deleted it. I typed another sentence. Backspace, backspace, backspace. My shoulders hunched. Was I getting a headache?

157

My throat felt tender. Maybe I should call, better yet email, the conference organizers and tell them I was sick.

Instead, I checked the morning headlines on MSNBC. com. The stock market . . . blah. Politics . . . Blah. Wait! What was this? *The 10 Sexiest Women over 40!*

I clicked the link. Jennifer Aniston, Vanessa Williams, some blond sports commentator I didn't recognize. The commentator wasn't nearly as pretty as the other over-forties; clearly the judges had just thrown her in as a token non-actress. In fact, I thought, I look as good as her, but just to be sure, I decided to do a quick check in the mirror.

My lord! No wonder I couldn't concentrate. Who could write with a face this tired? I tiptoed upstairs and retrieved my makeup bag from the master bathroom. While I was at it, I grabbed a handful of beauty products from a bottom drawer—bronzer, lip plumper, glitter-blue eye shadow. These were items I had bought on impulse over the years but rarely, if ever, used.

"What are you doing?" the Light Sleeper, mumbled from our bed. I had dropped the eyelash curler on my way to the stairs.

"I'm working," I snapped. "Go back to sleep." What did a person have to do around here to get a little quiet time to write?

By the time I finished my beauty makeover, and started a load of wash, the clock on my computer read 5:56 a.m. What had happened to the last two hours?

How to Help Students Write More, Write Better, and Be Happier. I stared at the screen. Not a single idea came to mind. Plus, it didn't help that now I was over-caffeinated, my eyelids felt glittery, and my lips were swollen from the plumper that had come with a page of consumer warnings. To settle myself down, I decided to reread an article I had recently sold to *The Writer* magazine. That was coherent, I thought, prompting me to reread some of my published essays, and then my more entertaining "sent" emails. Clearly, I used to be able to write, I reasoned. And if I did it before, I could do it again!

But first I needed to pee.

In the downstairs bathroom, I couldn't help but notice that the water in the toilet bowl was rippling. While this was more perplexing than worrisome, I hesitated to sit down, recalling stories of alligators in the sewers that occasionally swim up into people's toilets. Could there be a more humiliating way to die, I reflected, than to be eaten by an alligator while sitting on the toilet?

A clunking sounded through the wall. The bathroom floor started to shake, and the water in the toilet bowl rippled more discernibly. Oh, I caught on. Our wash machine in the adjoining laundry room — off balance for months — must have entered its final spin cycle. But hadn't I just started that load?

Back at the computer, the clock read 6:41 a.m. That left just one hour and nineteen minutes to write my talk, take a shower, and be on the road.

Steve came into the room, handing me a plate of toast. "How's it going?" he asked.

"I haven't written a word," I glared. "I'm doomed."

"You'll think of something," he said. "You always do."

How to Write More, Write Better, and Be Happier. When my own workshop participants are stuck, I give them a writing prompt to help them get started. Sometimes I tell them simply to start with a list.

"*One*," I typed, *Appreciate the value of bad writing. At least it's better than a blank page.*Oh puh-leeze, I thought, but made myself push on.

"*Two . . .*" An email for a male enhancement product popped onto my screen. I pressed delete, but it occurred to me: What if someone invented a real male enhancement product, but then no one would believe them because of all the spammers and pervs?

"*Two . . .*" I refocused. *Enhance your students' abilities by pointing out what is already working in their writing and why.*

"*Three . . .*" I took a bite of toast and smiled. *Have faith in every student, because even a little positive feedback can make a big difference.*

Forty minutes later, my talk was drafted, albeit rough in certain sections. Of course, now I had no time to rework it or make additions, despite one of the most important points I wanted to share with teachers—that writing is mostly rewriting.

7:42 a.m. I raced upstairs to the shower. En route, I grabbed the bar of exfoliating soap I had discovered earlier in the bathroom drawer. Yes, it occurred to me, as I scrubbed at the make-up on my face, careful to avoid my still-puffy lips, there indeed was a more humiliating way to die than to be attacked by an alligator while sitting on the toilet. You could be attacked by an alligator while sitting on the toilet while wearing glitter-blue eye shadow.

WINNING THE LOTTERY

The same day I got fired from my job as an advertising copy-writer, I had my second miscarriage. I don't believe there was any connection between these two events, other than some cosmic wise-guy's idea of a bad joke. Still, the timing gave me pause.

Most women rely on home pregnancy kits to verify conception, and I'd availed myself of two different brands just to be certain. But I also had my own way of reassuring myself that this pregnancy—which occurred about a year after my first miscarriage—was progressing. I simply ran up and down the stairs, as a means of seeing whether my breasts felt weird. Not painful really, but noticeable, given that under normal circumstances thoughts like—*Oh, my goodness, I'm certainly aware of my breasts today*—rarely, if ever, occurred to me.

That morning, however, when I'd hurried up and down our steps several times, worried I'd be late for work yet again, I didn't notice my breasts even once. This, I knew, was not a good sign.

I was a talented copywriter, but a terrible employee. First of all, like nine out of ten copywriters on the planet, I harbored dreams of becoming a famous author. At the time, short story writer Tama Janowitz was my standard for success, as much for her cool name and artsy New York City vibe as for the power of her prose. I was sure I could exude an artsy New York City vibe, if my name wasn't a relic of the Eisenhower era and I wasn't stuck writing brochures for the locally owned bank.

While my artistic pretensions didn't win me any points with my boss, more problematic was the fact that I spent a good part of each workday goofing off. In my defense, there wasn't much work to do, thanks to a recession that had motivated a lot of clients to cut their advertising budgets. But even when I worked at agencies during boom years, I was the kind of employee who trawled co-workers offices, hoping for entertainment and opportunities to pry into their personal lives.

At this particular agency, most of my time was spent gabbing with the art director, a kindred spirit, though his ambitions lay in creating weird paintings and art objects rather than hip short stories. How could I not want to spend all day hanging out with a guy who packaged little bottles of "holy water" with labels he designed depicting Elvis super-imposed on the Shroud of Turin?

And then there were other transgressions, like my liberal use of the copier for personal projects, and taking long lunches to allow for a shower after my mid-day workouts. (But really, why hurry back only to try and look busy?) My easy-going boss, George, seemed willing to ignore these offenses, but not so the agency's bookkeeper, a ruddy-cheeked woman with a tight perm and tighter fists. She made it abundantly clear that she was on to me, and while she had no authority over me or the creative department, she wielded her limited power by giving up our bi-weekly paychecks about as eagerly as a buzzard releases carrion.

Given my poor attitude and behavior, it was obvious even to me that my boss should have fired me months before he actually got around to it. Or I should have had the good graces to quit. But a paycheck is a paycheck, and with a baby coming in about seven months, knock on wood, my preference was to leave the job not as a quitter, but as a new mother wanting to

devote herself fully to her child. Of course, being an unem-
ployed mom was not feasible, given our financial situation,
nor had it ever been a particular ambition of mine. At the
time, however, all I knew was that I wanted this baby more
than anything in the world.

"I'd like to take you to lunch today." George announced
to me on this particular morning. "Do you have time around
noon?" Was he being sarcastic? He had found me, as usual,
hanging out in the art department. As soon as I saw him
approach, I pretended to be discussing some layout with
the designer.

"Uh, sure." This was the first of never. To date, our
socializing had been limited to him insisting on telling me
jokes about dumb blondes and gays. I could never really
tell if his affinity for this type of humor meant he actually
was sexist and homophobic, or just clueless, given that some
comic material is clearly better left untapped by straight
male bosses.

As the morning wore on, even more tedious than most,
I occupied myself by finding excuses to walk up and down
the agency steps, hoping for some signs of reassurance, and
debating with the art director the meaning behind my boss's
invitation. Could I really be getting the ax? But who takes
someone to lunch just to fire them? Answer: The same type
of boss who thinks it's appropriate to affect a lisp and limp
wrist as part of his regular stand-up routine at client meetings.

"I've changed my mind. I don't want to go to lunch."
Shortly before noon I went into my boss's office and bagged
out of his invitation. By now I felt certain of two things.
One: I didn't want to be eating some Caesar salad while
hearing all about my failings as an employee. And two: I
didn't want to be eating a Caesar salad at all, given that I
felt like crying. But this emotion had little to do with my job

situation, and everything to do with my suspiciously quiescent breasts, as well as other worrisome symptoms that had begun to show themselves.

"Fine," George shrugged. "We'll talk when I get back."

Fine! I imagined myself responding. *Just know that I'm pregnant and probably having a miscarriage.* Of course I didn't say this aloud. I'm not the type of person who can pull off this kind of soap opera dialogue with dignity. But also it felt disloyal to the baby. Was this what people meant by maternal instincts? The fates had handed me the perfect guilt-inducing card, yet I didn't want to play it if it meant exploiting my child.

After my boss took off for lunch, I sneaked into his office (first making sure the buzzard wasn't anywhere around), and confirmed my suspicions. My "Letter of Termination" rested face down on his desk, the header a cruel double entendre. Mercifully, it cited just one offense: I had misspelled the word "tomorrow" in a headline. Normally, this kind of careless mistake would have stung my professional pride, but at the moment my only reaction was, *Who cares about stupid tomorrow?*

I was thirty-seven and had been married for almost ten years when my husband and I finally got around to trying to conceive a child. This delay wasn't because I had mapped out my life, say, wanting to get established in my career before starting a family. Rather it was more like that refrigerator magnet with the image of a forty-something woman wearing a shocked expression on her face. "OMG," the caption reads, "I forgot to have children."

Because my biological clock was approaching last call when we started trying to conceive, one miscarriage, and then a second, brought with it the fear that soon enough I would either be unable to get pregnant, or I would simply run out of time before my body figured out how to make another pregnancy stick. For me, this second scenario was the less palatable one, maybe because it is one thing to have been screwed by the fates who determine conception, but quite another to have screwed yourself (absolutely no pun intended).

The afternoon I got fired from my advertising job, I went home, changed into sweatpants and one of my husband's flannel shirts, and then sat in a recliner with a blanket over my head. Sunlight filtered through the loose cream-colored weave. The cocoon made it easier to shut out the reality of losing another baby.

Only it wasn't a baby, I reminded myself, remembering how the doctor who had treated me after my first miscarriage seemed to avoid that tender word. "Most likely a chromosomal abnormality," she gently explained.

Apparently most early miscarriages are simply random, isolated events, a "medical mystery," as the doctor put it, too common to merit further testing, even in our country's test-happy, fee-for-service medical model.

"Maybe it's for the best," well meaning outsiders have been known to comment in these situations. No doubt, they're considering the alternative, such as giving birth to a mutant with two heads or six extra pairs of feet. I'm not offended by their logic, knowing their words are meant to comfort. And goodness knows my slacker-mother tendencies were much relieved when the children I eventually did give birth to became capable of brushing their own teeth and feeding themselves. But still, for the best?

About a year after I was fired, I found myself once again working at the same advertising agency, and once again two months pregnant. It was like déjà vu all over again, including the fact that I didn't want to divulge my condition until I was at least in my second trimester. If something should go wrong again, I wanted to deal with my grief privately.

George had invited me to return to my old job (with no mention of our past troubles) because business had picked up and he liked my copywriting style. In turn, I had agreed to come back because, while I totally preferred the life of a freelancer, self-employment had provided me with a new respect for a steady paycheck.

And now our small agency had been invited to pitch the New Hampshire State Lottery account! We worked for weeks on our creative strategy, media plan, and sample campaigns. I wished George's excitement at this opportunity would rub off on me, knowing that if we became the lottery's agency of record, it would be a windfall for our small firm. But secretly my feeling was that the only thing worse than having to look busy as a copywriter, was to actually be busy, always having to come up with creative new ways to get people to spend money on games of chance with impossible odds, and to do so while playing responsibly.

Ten minutes before our presentation was to begin, I found myself in the ladies' room of the State Lottery Commission's office, in a panic over whether I needed to throw up. With this pregnancy, unlike the previous two, came a good deal of morning sickness, and this queasiness was exacerbated by the fact that my dress—held together in the front by a long vertical row of ball-shaped buttons—was squeezing my thickened frame like a sausage casing.

Knowing that time was running out, I decided to take matters in my own hands. If I vomited now, this might allow me a reprieve from morning-sickness during the scheduled hour-long presentation. With this reasoning, I went into a stall, leaned over the toilet, and tried to make myself gag. This failed to achieve the intended effect, but the effort strained my dress to the bursting point. Tiny buttons popped forth, falling scattershot to the floor. Looking down, I discovered that my dress was gaping open across the chest, a sight at once horrifying and strangely gratifying. How was I supposed to leave the ladies' room in such a state of undress, let alone give a presentation? On the other hand, the display was even more reassuring than the step test. Clearly, my breasts were making themselves noticed, by me and soon enough by the three men and one woman who comprised the lottery commission.

In a panic, I started crawling around the bathroom tiles, frantically chasing down buttons. How this would remedy the situation I had no idea, given that I had no means of sewing the buttons back on. While I was on my hands and knees, the agency's account executive entered the bathroom. "Are you all right?" she asked. "George asked me to come get you." By now, I could only assume he must be apoplectic about my prolonged disappearance.

"I'm pregnant," I reluctantly volunteered. What choice did I have, given my compromising situation? This was not how I envisioned telling my coworkers my big news. If and when that time came, I fantasized a quietly triumphant disclosure. *I'm with child*, I would murmur, basking in my Madonna-esque glow, my hands cupping my rounded belly. What would be understood but remain unspoken was the joyful coda to this news — and, finally, thank God, I have a legitimate excuse to quit this job!

"Congratulations," the account executive offered, and to her credit she refrained from any further commentary. A transplanted Southerner, the woman had always fit my stereotype of a Steel Magnolia — gracious, fearless, and in possession of a designer handbag capacious enough to hold everything from bourbon, to charger plates, to a pearl- handled revolver. From this bag, she extracted a small plastic box with an array of safety pins, which she efficiently used to fasten me mostly back together.

We met George in the hallway and hurried into the conference room. En route, I felt compelled to tell him my situation, in case I needed to bolt for the bathroom. In response, he placed a trash can by my feet at the presentation table, a gesture that made up for every tasteless joke he had ever told.

In the end, we didn't get the lottery account, though our presentation went off without a hitch. But to capitalize on an obvious metaphor, I hit the jackpot. Not only did my lottery baby make it, but less than two years later I brought a second daughter into this world. Both my girls are perfect, of course. I say this in the same way that game show contestants always seem to introduce themselves on TV, *"Yes, Pat, I'm married with two beautiful children."* Just looking at some of those contestants, you know their children can't all be beautiful. But I get it. A parent sees what no one else can see.

Even after all these years, even as I celebrate my amazing good fortune as a mother, I still feel the loss of those first two pregnancies. I understand the logic of chromosomal abnormalities and how those babies—as babies—existed more in my head than in fact. But sometimes wishful thinking prevails over logic, which explains why those unborn babies remain so real to me, and, come to think of it, why so many people play the lottery.

Given that I take no comfort in the concept of cosmic wise-guys, or random, isolated events for that matter, I have had to come to terms with those miscarriages in my own illogical way. And so here is one medical mystery resolved, compliments of my abilities as a talented copywriter to sell almost anything, at least to myself.

Those first two babies simply chose to live somewhere else; let's say a big, fluffy cumulous cloud where they and all the other babies who were never born are not just viable but happy. In my mind's eye I can see them now, smiling and waving down at me, kicking soccer balls with their extra feet, and looking so beautiful, so perfect, I could almost cry.

BREAKING DAWN

I like to think that the family I grew up in wouldn't fit in with the type of people who appear on all those judge shows my mother used to watch on TV. My family is well educated, morally superior—we work as teachers, writers, wire-tapping specialists. When I watched the judge shows with my mom, and listened to the disputants argue their cases, all I could think was, *How stupid can you be? If you're going to allow your deadbeat ex-lover to crash at your apartment after his landlord gives him the boot, then you deserve to be out the damages when his pit bull chews up your X-box.*

"Why do you watch this stuff?" I asked my mom during one of my visits. Judge Judy was presiding over the case of the New Jersey exterminator who accused one of his clients of throwing a brick at his van, causing him undue stress.

"Bullshit," my mom had responded, not to me but to the television. According to the defendant, he wasn't aiming the brick at the van; the van just happened to drive-by when he threw it. My mom was not a lawyer, but she was a first-grade teacher for over thirty years, making her equally, if not more qualified than Judge Judy to see through the lame excuses of immature criminals.

Because my mother was never a sap, and because she had been witness to hundreds of televised court cases since advancing age and decrepitude confined her to her recliner, this makes the case of Dawn versus my family all the more perplexing.

Dawn was one of a roster of home health aides who came to my mom's house to make sure that she and her two dogs didn't have to go to a nursing home. Dawn wasn't from the "Visiting Angels" agency my family relied on to guarantee round-the-clock assistance. Dawn was an independent hire, brought in several days a week to provide some continuity of care and companionship.

Dawn—Caucasian, sun-leathered, fortyish, full of manic energy and celebrity gossip—seemed like a good fit for my mom, and not just because English was her first language. Unlike a lot of the Visiting Angels who sit quietly and do paperwork and exude a Bible-study-group vibe, Dawn was fun. She liked to talk back to the TV and drink box wine, just like my mom. They went places—A.C. Moore, Yankee Candle, the mall. They even had Lucy-and-Ethel like adventures, like the time they stole an Obama-for-President sign from someone's front yard, and their crime (unsolved) made the evening news.

Dawn worked for my mother for over a year and was, by far, her favorite caregiver, more like a friend than an employee. Unfortunately, Dawn was also a liar, a thief, and a drug addict.

This was not just my family's opinion, but also that of my mother's cleaning lady, Jane. At one point, Jane and Dawn had been best buddies (in fact, Dawn was the one who had recommended Jane to my mother), but then they'd had one of those falling-outs so common among thieves, and Jane started snitching on Dawn.

Here, I should add that Jane had her own criminal tendencies, like asking my mother for cash advances, then failing to remind her of this come payday, thus taking advantage of an old woman's lapses in short-term memory, as well as her fear of losing a good housecleaner. Still, my sister believed Jane when she ratted out Dawn, mostly because it confirmed our family's own suspicions.

Dawn was stealing from my mother, if not always by pocketing cash, then in sneakier ways. Armed with my mom's ATM card and PIN number, Dawn withdrew hundreds, sometimes thousands of dollars a week from my mom's checking account, all with my mom's blessing. While part of Dawn's job was to curb my mom's increasing bouts of compulsive spending, instead she took advantage of this cloud cover of consumption, presumably in the hopes that it would obscure her own siphoning off of the spoils.

Who was to say whether my mom needed yet another dozen collared sweatshirts sporting images of cardinals or kittens, or that second ruby ring, or those hard-cover mystery books that she no longer could see to read? But what about all those miracle anti-aging creams that she didn't even remember ordering? Or the Costco-size party platters that mysteriously came and went from my mom's refrigerator? Or those sixty-eight dollar Victoria Secret's "invisible" push up bras, consisting of nothing more than two self-adhesive silicone cups?

It happened to be me, home on a visit, who found the Victoria Secret bras (what there was of them), still nestled in their egg-shaped packages, just biding their time in an out- of-the-way closet. The bras, a generous C cup, were useless to my mom with her collared sweatshirts, but just the right size and level of trampy-ness for the well-endowed Dawn.

Something had to be done.

Like all things related to my mom's care, it fell to Jeanne, the oldest among us five children, and the only one who still lived in our hometown, to fire Dawn when the obvious could no longer be ignored.

The reaction was swift and brutal.

Dawn to my mom (calling several times a day): "Your daughter says we can't be friends any more. She won't let me see you!"

My mom to me: "Goddamnit!" (I cringed, thinking of the newest Visiting Angel overhearing such language.) "Your sister thinks she can tell me what to do with my life! I'm calling my lawyer! Whose money is it anyway?"

My sister to me: "What was I supposed to do? The woman was a thief!"

Oh boy. I settled into my chair next to the phone. When it came to managing my mom's care, Jeanne's role was to take on all the responsibility, then bear the brunt of our mother's displaced anger at being incapacitated and dependent. My role, as the youngest daughter who did nothing and was hence immune from my mother's wrath, was to listen to my sister rail about this injustice for as long as she wanted.

Three weeks after Jeanne fired Dawn, she rehired her, caving under my mother's relentless anger and tears. Like all five of us grown children, Jeanne had almost come to terms with the fact that our mother seemed to prefer her obnoxious dog over us. Still, it proved too much for her to accept that some white trash con artist had supplanted her in our mother's affections, as well.

Fortunately, Dawn's second stint as my mother's caregiver only lasted a few more months. Dawn began helping my mom spend her money with such abandon (More beauty products! Furniture! Car shopping!) that even the unassuming Visiting Angels felt compelled to report her behavior. What's more, Jane, the housekeeper, squealed to my sister that Dawn had started leaving my mom alone while she ran errands. And those two weeks Dawn had suddenly needed off for a family emergency? She was really in court-ordered rehab.

The second time Jeanne fired Dawn, the reaction was surprisingly quiet.

Dawn called my sister and threatened to sue her for something or other, no doubt inspired by all those hours she spent by my mother's side watching Court TV. She also tried to reach my mom a few times, but the other caregivers—and the specter of the Office of Aging—kept her at bay.

I called my mom, who mentioned briefly, "I think Dawn was stealing from me. Your sister had to fire her." (And just like that, she had dismissed Dawn from her life, eventually finding a new—and thankfully law-abiding—favorite caretaker.)

Meanwhile, my sister and I still talk occasionally about Dawn, asking ourselves and each other, "How stupid could we be to let a crook take care of our mother?"

But now, of course, I have learned that not being stupid isn't always that easy. I'm sure if my sister and I appeared on one of the judge shows my mom loved to watch, viewers like me would have had a field day. *Those daughters gave that woman their mom's PIN number?! She was draining her savings for God's sake! And to make matters worse, they hired her not once but twice!*

On the other hand, I could make the case that Dawn was my mother's crazy friend—and everybody needs a crazy friend. So what if she let my mom spend money on things she could no longer use. So what if she lied and stole along the way. If I was dependent on round-the-clock care, how much would I pay for some fun? How much would I spend for a semblance of control, for the illusion that I could turn back the clock?

Reality or no, Dawn and my mother were Ethel and Lucy, still having adventures long after the show was canceled. And like my mom used to yell when she wanted what she wanted, "Whose money is it anyway?"

WALKING THE LABYRINTH

I am standing in my stocking feet in a college gymnasium, about to "walk the labyrinth" with a dozen or so conference goers. I came to this conference to teach a writing workshop, but afterwards the organizer invited me to participate in the other activities, all geared toward personal transformation and spiritual growth. I wanted to cut out early—do some Christmas shopping and take the afternoon off—but what does that say about me? Nothing I'd care to hear, I'm sure.

This particular "labyrinth" is a circle painted on a drop cloth that covers half the gym floor. The purple lines on the labyrinth create a circuitous path that, according to Labyrinth Lady, our leader in this exercise, represents a spiritual pathway. "Think of it as a walking prayer or meditation," Labyrinth Lady tells our small group. "A metaphoric journey to the deepest center of your self."

The gym falls quiet, too quiet, save for a strain of flute-y music coming from the CD player on the bleachers. We are to begin our journey when we feel ready, entering the labyrinth in measured intervals. "Be attentive; open to the experience," Labyrinth Lady has instructed. "You only have to enter and follow the path."

The Weeper, of course, goes first, just as she was the first to volunteer to read her writing in my workshop. In this conference full of touchy-feely types, The Weeper takes the prize for over-shares. Next goes Yoga Ono, (Oh, yes, I have made up names for everyone at the conference), then Mother Earth, who presses her palms together and bows her head before stepping onto the drop cloth.

I am struck, once again, by Mother Earth's giant owl necklace made of wire mesh and feathers with a Double D wingspan. She designed the piece herself, as part of her sacred symbol line of jewelry that she sells online. When I first saw the necklace, I thought it was so ugly I felt compelled to gush over it with such conviction that we both agreed I should be on her emailing list.

I bide my time as a few more walkers enter the labyrinth, my goal being to insert myself somewhere in the middle of the group. I wish I was anywhere but here. Spiritual paths, sacred symbols, music with wooden flutes—I can't relate to any of this.

Now!

I make my move, cutting off the Administrative Assistant from a Small Midwestern University who has approached the labyrinth at the same time as me. I don't know if this woman actually is an administrative assistant from a small Midwestern university but she fits the stereotype, hence I have dubbed her as such. "Sorry," I mouth to her, but refuse to give way. Like the rest of the world, I have no trouble taking advantage of low-level administrators.

In the labyrinth, I remind myself to be open to the experience; to journey to the center of my self. But try as I might, I can be neither introspective nor even focused, partly because of all the purple paint splatters outside the lines on the drop cloth. You would have thought that the painters would have done a better job, especially given that this labyrinth is supposed to look like the famous one in Chartres Cathedral.

Splat! Splat! Why is Labyrinth Lady so fat? Every time I see another splatter, this ditty pops into my head. This is what always happens to me when I try to be spiritual; my mind automatically goes in the opposite direction. I become the Maker Funner, and I can't stand maker funners.

Time drags. Eventually the walkers become spread out through the labyrinth. Some meander at a solemn pace; others skip or sway. Occasionally two walkers hug spontaneously when crossing paths. This is exactly the kind of behavior the conference organizers have encouraged, with no regard for personal space. Earlier in the day, I was hiding in the back of a presentation on Singing Your Peace, hoping against hope that the workshop leader wouldn't notice me, when a frail, bald woman approached me.

"Can I rub your back?" she whispered. "You look tense."

You can't be serious? I thought. But instead of saying no, I smiled and nodded. The last thing I wanted was for this poor woman to assume that I was one of those awful people who thinks cancer is contagious. Determined to help me relax, she kept rubbing and rubbing my shoulders until, thankfully, her strength gave out, right before my trapezoids strangled one another.

The center of the labyrinth is painted in a rosette design, the symbol of enlightenment, among other things.

Labyrinth Lady has told us to pause here; to reflect or pray or give thanks. Big things can happen in the center, she intimated. I watch the others who arrive before me. Yoga Ono stretches her arms toward the beam of light funneling through one of the high, gym windows. The Administrative Assistant from the Small Midwestern University twirls with abandon. The Weeper, of course, is weeping.

Oh, give it a rest, I snap at her silently. Why do you have to be such a bawl baby? But by now I am near tears myself. When I reach the rosette I feel nothing even remotely profound. What is wrong with me? I think. Why is everyone else so good at walking the labyrinth? Was I behind the door when God handed out sacred symbols? On the way out of the labyrinth I cross paths once again with Mother Earth and her giant owl necklace. We smile and she engulfs me in a hug, she likely thinking enlightened thoughts; me thinking, I can't wait to hit unsubscribe.

On my way home from the conference, I stop at the mall around dusk. Better late than never, I think, wishing I had made my escape hours ago. The outside of the building twinkles with white lights. Inside, holiday music fills the air. I stroll down the aisles, admiring the festive decorations. Christmas is still ten days away, but one of the department stores is already having a sale on all seasonal items, so I buy a little snow globe to add to my growing collection.

The atrium of the mall has been converted into Santa's Village, replete with workshops for the elves and a sleigh where kids can sit on Santa's lap, at least during his working hours. I buy myself a soft pretzel and soda and sit at one of the nearby tables. At this hour the mall is fairly quiet and peaceful. It has been a long day and feels good to just be—to not have to keep pretending.

My new snow globe displays two tiny reindeers prancing around a Christmas tree. I turn it over and glittery snowflakes swirl throughout the glass. I love snow globes, the way the tiny scenes contained within them transport me to a miniature, magical world. I turn the globe over again, admiring the pretty effect. I used to believe the figures within snow globes came to life when no one was watching. Even now, I look at the one in my hands, hoping to catch a sign of movement.

I know I am not religious, at least not in the traditional sense. And, clearly, I am a failure at labyrinths. But it occurs to me now, sitting in the middle of this mall, right next to Santa's village and sleigh, that I do believe in miracles. I believe there are all sorts of spiritual pathways, including one for me. And I do have a sacred object. I turn the globe again and watch as the snow settles over the reindeer. Indeed, I realize, I have a whole collection of them.

THE YEAR OF THE DOG

According to the Chinese zodiac, I was born in the Year of the Dog, a fact I learned from a paper placemat at an all-you-can-eat buffet. You would think this would have thrilled me, given that I'm a dog freak. And by freak I don't just mean that I anthropomorphize my own precious Chihuahua mutt, a little-big man who loves his human Mommy sooo much.

No, I get mushy hearted when I lay eyes on any dog—snorting pugs and leaping Labs (too cute), mixed breeds like Labradoodles and Bassetcats that defy the laws of nature (so precious), even my neighbor's dog from childhood, a scruffy-haired mutt named Fred who chased me back to my own yard, where I fell while scrambling over our patio wall and ended up scarred for life.

Just like every other true dog freak in the world, I simply can't resist accosting dog-walkers in the street, asking to pet their pooches. A similar feeling overtakes me in parking lots, whenever I see a dog waiting behind the steering wheel for its owner to return from Pet-Smart or the grocery store or the casino. If my daughters are with me, I feel compelled to draw their attention to this adorable scenario, "Look! Look, girls! Isn't that precious, a Rottweiler driving the car!" Then I wave and shout baby-talk at it through the cracked-open window, until the formerly calm dog goes berserk, trying to leap through the glass, either to frolic or to kill this strange lady in the parking lot.

Given my freakish love of dogs, it took me by surprise when my immediate reaction to my Chinese zodiac sign was…what? Disappointment? Peevishness? An urge to snap at someone? The feeling was similar to when I was a little girl and fantasized that my real parents were royalty from a magical kingdom. Then I looked in the mirror and saw my father's entire side of the family looking back at me, and had to face the disappointing truth. I simply came from loving, hard-working, oppression-fleeing Eastern Europeans with droopy eyelids and ridiculously large earlobes.

The placemat noted that people born in the Year of the Dog possess the best attributes of human nature. They have a deep sense of loyalty. They are honest. They inspire other people's confidence because they know how to keep secrets. In addition to those stellar qualities, being a dog just sounds better than some of the other choices in the Chinese zodiac. People born in the Year of the Rat, for example, also are credited with positive attributes—they're ambitious, and industrious—but then there's that whole bubonic plague thing, which can't be overlooked.

So what was it about my Chinese zodiac sign that prickled me? If I had been seeing a therapist at the time, I could have discussed my vague, discordant feelings for hours, or at least until my insurance coverage ran out. That's what I did in an attempt to come to terms with Western astrology, which denotes me as a Pisces, the water sign, despite my aversion to swimming and beach vacations. In junior high, where learning to swim in the school pool was a required humiliation, I couldn't even master the dead man's float. At the time, I rationalized that this was because I lacked the percentage of body fat required for buoyancy. (Oh, to have those problems now!) But this didn't explain why I also couldn't turn a cartwheel or, for that matter, why I hated people touching my hair, or why I constantly licked my lips. Eventually, it was a simple word association game— equally useful for breaking the ice at parties and conducting psychiatric evaluations—that illuminated my problem with being born in the Year of the Dog. In case you have never been to a lame party or had a psychiatric evaluation, here is how word association works.

I say the word *lilac*, for example. Now you respond with the first word that comes to mind. Then I repeat the same word to probe further, or follow up with another related or random word. For instance, I might say *pillow* or *marginalia* or *grandma*. It really doesn't matter because when you word associate there are no wrong responses, that is unless your uniform response to every word is *bloodbath*, in which case you are likely a psycho or should stop watching Quentin Tarantino movies on high definition TV. But either way, you will have gained self knowledge, and that is always a good thing.

Below is a re-creation of my own experience when I played the word association game, in an effort to get to the bottom of my discomfiture with my Chinese zodiac sign.

Dog.
Adorable-Cuddly-Precious!

While I *wished* I possessed those attributes, none of them stirred any disturbing emotions in me, other than a desire to find my own little big-man wherever he was hiding, and kiss him all over his fuzzy head.

Dog.
Domesticated.

Dog.
Loyal.

Ah, here I did feel some flutters of disquiet. But loyalty is a good thing, right? Whoever invented the Chinese Zodiac seemed to think so, as do most people. Loyalty, after all, is one of the main reasons we dog freaks love our dogs. Think about the true story of that famous Akita named Hachikō, who waited at the train station every day for his master to return home from work. In fact, Hachikō was such a loyal dog he continued to meet the train every afternoon for nine years *after* his master died. Then, when Hachikō also died, the train station erected a statue of him. Whose nose doesn't sting just thinking about that bizarrely touching story?

And, of course, loyalty in humans is an equally admirable trait. Without loyalty, people wouldn't have lasting or meaningful relationships. We also wouldn't have incentive programs like frequent flyer miles or guest rewards. And we certainly wouldn't have any Chicago Cubs fans. But then again, when I thought of loyalty, I also thought of an old friend of mine I'll call Mary, whom I knew when I lived in Philadelphia.

When Mary and I were in our late twenties, we found ourselves in similar circumstances when each of our fairly new boyfriends moved out of state (hers to California, mine to Minnesota). Note, I'm using the term "boyfriends" loosely, given that neither of us had been dating these men long enough to secure a commitment. Regardless, as a result of their moves, both of us suddenly found ourselves in that cruel limbo of "what ifs" and "what nows," more commonly known as the long-distance relationship.

For Mary, having a long-distance boyfriend meant spending Friday and Saturday nights in her apartment, relentlessly replaying Karla Bonoff albums. If she did venture out to socialize, she usually wore bib overalls, indisputably one of the most powerful defenses against male advances, sexual or conversational. In this way she remained loyal to the man with whom she hoped to share a future.

I also had strong feelings for my long-distance boyfriend (feelings that ranged from maybe-love to irritation that he would inconvenience me by moving away). Unlike Mary, however, I continued to date and go out on weekends. (And I must say I looked hot in my harem jeans and off-the-shoulder Flash Dance sweaters.) It made no sense to close myself off to other opportunities, I reasoned, especially while my unclothed body still looked fairly good in dim lights. Eight seasons of field hockey throughout high school and college had earned me those firm thighs, and it just seemed wrong to squander the few good years left on them waiting at home for a sign from the Midwest.

But was I being disloyal? I often found myself debating the integrity of my behavior, especially in comparison to Mary's unwavering display of devotion. Then again, I would bristle, her self sacrifice struck me more as weak than virtuous. It has always left me cold, when women pine for elusive men. Love them, of course, if it can't be helped (I certainly knew that feeling), but for goodness sakes, stop behaving like a martyr, wearing out your vinyl records.

In the end it was a moot point, whether Mary or I had the right attitude toward love. Within a year we both had married our long-distance boyfriends, and are still married to them. Twenty-five years later, I know that loyalty is the cornerstone of my enduring marriage, of any marriage, really...that is until I turn on the TV and see yet another wife, one not so lucky in love, standing by her man as he apologizes for his multiple affairs, and, oh, by the way, he is indeed the father of his assistant's baby, a fact he admits, but only after being shamed into submitting to DNA testing.

Dog.
Obedient.

Dog.
Work like a dog.

These last associations brought to mind a tour I'd taken with
my family to the first commercial pretzel bakery in America,
established in 1861. We were among a small crowd of visitors,
including children on a field trip from a nearby Mennonite
elementary school. All of us gathered around a long table in
the original bakery, eager to get a hands-on lesson in pretzel
twisting.

"When the bakery first opened," our guide, a jovial,
big-bellied retiree smiled, "twenty women stood around this
very same table, working six days a week, ten hours a day,
twisting pretzels." As he talked, he divided a pile of rather
grey pretzel dough into small sections for each of us.

"Who can tell me what this instrument is for?" The guide
gestured to a huge wooden paddle near a barrel marked flour.
It seemed obvious that the heavy board was for mixing large
batches of dough, but I didn't speak up because the question
was clearly intended for the children in the audience. My
own daughters, who hadn't been too keen on taking this tour
in the first place, remained silent, as did the well behaved
Mennonites.

"Okay, I'll tell you," our guide winked at a little girl with
long blond braids capped by a lace head covering. "This giant
paddle was too keep the women who worked here in line."
He chuckled and made a smacking motion with his hand.

Was that supposed to be funny? I thought. Was this some
kind of twisted pretzel humor? Given the epidemic of violence against women around the world—especially against
younger women—this kind of cavalier joking only trivialized
the issue. I looked around to see mostly smiles or expressions
of boredom. Maybe I was over-reacting?

The guide went on to explain that pretzels were first invented around 600 AD by a monk who was working in the kitchen. He was playing around with his dough (now that statement begged a joke), when he happened to twist it into a form resembling arms crossed in prayer. Inspired by his design, he offered these baked *pretiolas* to children as a reward for their reverence.

"The women who worked here," the guide added in his cheerful manner, "were expected to twist fifty pretzels a minute."

"Were all the pretzel twisters women?" I asked, mostly out of curiosity, though I still felt vexed by his earlier comment. "Didn't any men have to twist fifty pretzels a minute for ten hours a day, six days a week?"

"Now why would a man work for just ten cents an hour?" This time the jolly fucker aimed his wink at me.

Dog.
Trained.

Dog.
Leash.

As in this recent comment from a friend of mine, "Boy, your husband sure gives you a long leash." My friend was inspired to say this after I went dancing two nights in a row without my spouse, a.k.a. the leash holder.

"I just like to dance more than he does," I explained, which was the truth. But after stewing about this comment for days, I realized what I really wanted to say was, *Are you kidding me? What century are we in? Since when does a wife need permission to go dancing?* And this thought opened up a floodgate of feminist indignation.

Why are some elected officials (male and female) determined to set back women's rights?

Why do female employees still earn less pay for equal work?
And why doesn't somebody slap Don Draper?

Of course, that last statement put me on par with the pretzel tour guide. But hear me out. For those of you who have never watched the TV series *Mad Men*, a show set in the early 1960s, Don Draper is the main character, a gorgeous, talented advertising executive who is also a sexist product of his times. He cheated on his wife before she left him, and keeps several mistresses. And while his attitude toward women at his firm isn't nearly as loathsome as that of some of his male co-workers, he still just doesn't get it.

Maybe because I worked in advertising for years and never liked it, or maybe because *Mad Men* is set in an era when housekeeping and raising a family were still considered ideal female roles, I find the show almost too irritating to watch. In fact, the few times I've tuned in, I have wanted to slap Don Draper myself, this despite the fact that his jaw line is made of granite. Of course that impulse is often followed by a mental image of him stopping my white-gloved hand mid-slap, and then lowering me to the conference table where we enjoy wild, consensual sex. But this only clarifies that it is not Don Draper's physical dominance that offends me, only his assumption that I should fetch him his coffee or that he, by virtue of his gender, can write better advertising copy than me.

By this point in the word association game, an obvious theme had emerged related to my feelings about the Chinese zodiac. Clearly, I concluded, being born in the Year of the Dog riled my feminist sensibilities. Yes, I loved dogs as pets, but I didn't want their most notable attributes—domesticated, obedient, waiting around for people who have been dead for nine years—to be my primary assets. Or was I just being snarky?

Dog.
Bitch.

Here was yet another one of my least favorite words, too often applied to any woman who exerts a strong voice or stands up for herself. That said, lately I've noticed that some women writers are co-opting the term for their own purposes. Looking for some tough love on how to lose weight and be healthy? Consult the best-selling book *Skinny Bitch*. Want to read about what women really think about their relationships? *Let The Bitch in the House* tell it to you straight. While I still can't get past the ugly tenor of that word, and prefer to think women can do better than resorting to a mood-swing mentality to communicate their wisdom, these authors did give me an idea.

If I have to be a dog, I thought, then why not redefine that label to my liking? Rather than resist my birthright, why not embrace it and capitalize on its strengths? After all, even in the Chinese Zodiac there has to be an alpha dog, and that is one label, I'll admit, that suits me just fine. With this broadened perspective, I realized that I didn't need to feel at odds with my birth year; I could move on and form new associations. In fact, I could imagine a whole new meaning for the Year of the Dog:

This is the year we eliminate sexism and gender discrimination.

This is the year we put a stop to domestic violence.

This is the year we never have to see another one of those liquor ads featuring a half naked woman draped over a tuxedo-clad male.

And so, as a self-proclaimed alpha dog, I invite everybody—not just those who share my sign in the Chinese zodiac, or all those other dog freaks like me, but also ambitious and industrious rats, jolly tour guides, and even Don Draper and cat people — to declare themselves honorary dogs. I know my idealistic vision of the Year of the Dog doesn't quite match the reality of the times, but we might as well keep the faith. Because as that statue of the loyal Hachikō serves to remind us, even if today doesn't bring us what we've been hoping and waiting for, there's always tomorrow, and the tomorrow after that.

ACKNOWLEDGMENTS

In one essay in this collection I make a comment about how gratitude lists get on my nerves. Yet as I sat down to write these acknowledgments, I started feeling weepy and sentimental before I had even typed a word.

Thank you to my editor, Jeremy Townsend, for believing in this book, and for laughing with me, not at me. I am also grateful to have my agent, Lisa Bankoff, in my corner, and for Anne Adams, editor of the *Valley News*, who indulged me with a newspaper column, despite my inability to meet word counts. I also want to say a special thank you to Nancy Fontaine, my part-time muse, part-time Web site creator, and full-time friend through many years and five books.

With much appreciation to Chris Demers, for her book design talents, her extraordinary patience, and her friendship. Also, a special thanks to Helmut Baer for designing my book cover, and for being my partner in love, life, and creativity.

Because most of the family I grew up with are the opposite of touchy feely, let me also take this opportunity here, at a comfortable distance, to say I love you to Jeanne, Jill, John, and Brian. And to my sister Jeanne, in particular, thank you for being there every day.

And to my parents, who gave me a childhood of heart-warming and hilarious bad-dog stories.

ABOUT THE AUTHOR

In work and life, author and writing teacher Joni B. Cole prefers a macro lens, seeking the extraordinary in the ordinary, the significance in everyday moments. She is the author of the acclaimed books *Good Naked: Reflections on How to Write More, Write Better, and Be Happier,* and *Toxic Feedback: Helping Writers Survive and Thrive.* Joni is also the creator of the three-volume "This Day" series that shares a day in the life of hundreds of women across America and from all walks of life ("fascinating and eye-opening," *Publisher's Weekly*). Joni leads creative writing workshops in the Master of Arts in Liberal Studies program at Dartmouth College and at her own Writer's Center in White River Junction, Vermont. She is also on the faculty of the New Hampshire Institute of Art, and leads expressive writing workshops at a diversity of nonprofit and educational organizations. For more info, email jonibethcole@gmail.com or visit jonibcole.com